THE EVENLODE

British Library Cataloguing-in-publication data.
A catalogue record for this book is available from the British Library.
ISBN 0 9526031 7 9

First published in 2004 by Green Branch Press, Kencot Lodge, Kencot, Lechlade, Gloucestershire GL7 3QX, United Kingdom. Tel. 01367 860588. Fax 01367 860619.

Typeset by Green Branch Press.

Printed and bound by Stoate and Bishop Printers, Cheltenham.

Cover picture: original painting by Dawn Niven

Maps: Pat Grover

The Evenlode

an exploration of a Cotswold river

By Gordon Ottewell

Best wishes!

Gordon Ottewell

Sept 2004

Green Branch

Details given in this book were accurate at the time of writing, and have been carefully checked. However, the publisher and author can accept no responsibility for unforeseen hazards or changes.

Contents

GENERAL INTRODUCTION 6

Index to Maps 10

Walk 1: LONGBOROUGH & BOURTON-ON-THE-HILL 12

Walk 2: EVENLODE VILLAGE CIRCULAR........................ 16

Walk 3: ADLESTROP, ODDINGTON & DAYLESFORD 20

Walk 4: KINGHAM & BLEDINGTON HEATH 24

Walk 5: BLEDINGTON & FOXHOLES.. 28

Walk 6: SHIPTON, LYNEHAM & BRUERN 32

Walk 7: SHIPTON & ASCOTT 36

Walk 8: ASCOTT, SHORTHAMPTON & CHILSON 40

Walk 9: CHARLBURY, DEAN GROVE & COLDRON MILL 44

Walk 10: CHARLBURY, CORNBURY & FAWLER 48

Walk 11: STONESFIELD & COMBE 52

Walk 12: THE GLYME VALLEY 56

Walk 13: BLENHEIM PARK 60

Walk 14: LONG HANBOROUGH CIRCULAR 64

Walk 15: CASSINGTON AND THE THAMES 68

The Evenlode and the railway 72

WORKS CONSULTED 73

Index 74

GENERAL INTRODUCTION

As is the case with many English rivers, pin-pointing the exact source of the River Evenlode is a hazardous exercise. Even the indispensable Ordnance Survey Outdoor Leisure 45 map, drawn to a scale of 2.5 inches to the mile (4 cm to 1 km) leaves room for speculation, showing numerous tiny watercourses converging on Moreton-in-Marsh from north and west, yet withholding acknowledgment of the actual existence of a river until an irregular yet clearly defined blue line is named a mile or more south of the town.

Like the other Thames tributaries draining the Cotswolds away to the west – Churn, Coln, Leach, Windrush – the Evenlode flows through a valley entirely disproportionate to its modest size. This is because at the time of the thawing of the glaciers, the valley was scoured by meltwaters from the ice sheets, which in time deposited layers of clays, sands and gravels. These in turn gave rise to the deciduous woodland and fertile farmland for which the Evenlode valley is noted.

from Drayton's 'Poly-Olbion', 1622

From these obscure and unremarkable beginnings, the Evenlode, fed by tributary streams from east and west, picks its way in a series of wriggles in a south-easterly direction, leaving Gloucestershire between Bledington and

Kingham to enter Oxfordshire. There follows a bold sweep eastwards, in which the maturing river describes a great curve around Wychwood Forest, passing Charlbury and shaking off the last remnants of the Cotswolds. The final phase of the Evenlode's career sees it weave a tortuous course south eastwards, capturing the little River Glyme as it does so before finally heading south to meet its destiny – the Thames – below Cassington, a mere 5 miles north west of the centre of Oxford.

The Evenlode received its present name—that of the village south of Moreton-in-Marsh—as late as the 16th century, having been recorded as Yenload on Michael Drayton's map in his Poly-Olbion of 1612. Previously, it had been known as the Bladen, and as such had given its name to Bledington and Bladon, two villages along its valley. A casual glance at the map reveals that the Evenlode is followed for all but the last three or so miles of its 30-odd mile course by a railway. This line, laid out originally by the celebrated Isambard Kingdom Brunel for the Oxford, Worcester and Wolverhampton Railway, opened in 1853, and still forms part of the Paddington-Hereford line, along which modern diesel trains provide a service once performed by the elegant and distinctive locomotives and rolling stock of the Great Western Railway.

Although the rail passenger is fortunate in being able to enjoy a succession of delightful close-quarters glimpses of the Evenlode, sadly the lack of public rights-of-way along much of its length restricts the walker to a limited number of such opportunities. Even so, it has been possible in this book to offer fifteen interesting and varied circular walks, making use of available footpaths and bridleways, wherever possible alongside or in close proximity to the river, and including some of the most attractive and historically significant villages along or close to the valley.

The countryside of the Evenlode valley has drawn a varying range of responses from writers over the years. The Oxford don William Warde Fowler, who lived in the Oxfordshire village of Kingham for many years, wrote in his *Kingham Old and New* (1913) of its 'healthy, breezy climate, which is cold without being too cold,' adding 'It is a delightful country for an active man to live in, whether he hunts or cycles, or humbly walks, as I do.'

Edward Thomas, who studied at Lincoln College during the time Warde Fowler was Sub Rector, described in a short mystical piece entitled *On the Evenlode* in his *Horae Solitariae* (1902) how he rose early one June morning and sculled in a dinghy for nearly two hours up the Evenlode before running aground on the pebbles of a shallow. He then ventured inland until 'The river was out of sight and even of hearing, for in summer it stole through the land like a dream.'

Hilaire Belloc, too, made his acquaintance with the Evenlode during his student days at Oxford. Calling it 'perfect' many years later in his *Dedicatory Ode*, he went on to praise it as:

A lovely river, all alone,
She lingers in the hills and holds
A hundred little towns of stone,
Forgotten in the western wolds.

H.J. Massingham, by contrast, while conceding that the Evenlode countryside was 'passably fair to outward view', went on in his *Wold Without End* (1932) to call the Evenlode 'The least attractive of the endearing Cotswold rivers.' Later, in *Cotswold Country* (1937), he elaborated at length on this opinion: 'Perhaps I am fanciful in sensing a kind of impalpable sadness along the eastern border of the Cotswolds……. I have always felt a certain mournfulness about it………. I feel that an invisible mist of regret overhangs the Valley of the Evenlode.'

The increasing use of alien building materials contributed to Massingham's misgivings, together with what he saw as the sombre influence of Wychwood Forest. He went on to quote the assertion made about the Evenlode valley by a Chipping Campden farmer: 'Oh ay, the land be bewitched; it be full of devils.'

Leaving aside these quaint superstitions, there is no denying that the Evenlode possesses a quality aptly described by an alternative definition of the verb to bewitch, namely to delight exceedingly. And as the discerning walker will find, the many delights to be savoured along its valley offer ample reward for the time and effort spent.

Each of the itineraries is preceded by an introduction covering matters such as archaeology, buildings, history, natural features, traditions, literary associations, and the natural history of the Evenlode Valley.

ACKNOWLEDGEMENTS

I should like to thank the following people and organisations who helped with this book:-

Christopher and Caroline Yapp, Anne Harvey, and Patty and Peter Stone, who walked many of the routes with me and in so doing provided good company and many helpful suggestions.

Dawn Niven, for producing a cover that catches the character of the River Evenlode so perfectly.

The staff of Winchcombe, Witney, Milton-under-Wychwood and Stow in the Wold libraries for all their advice and assistance.

Ron Prew, Curator of the Charlbury Museum, for the loan of photographs of old Charlbury.

Mr & Mrs P.M.Mercer, for temporarily replacing the Hamo Thorneycroft statue in its former niche and allowing it to be photographed.

Margaret, my wife, for her practical help and support throughout.

Finally, I wish it to be known that any mistakes, omissions or other shortcomings the book may have are mine and mine alone.

Gordon Ottewell

March 2004

Index to Maps

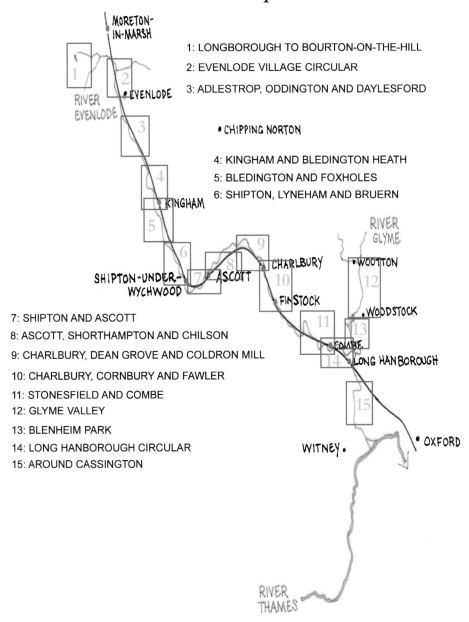

1: LONGBOROUGH TO BOURTON-ON-THE-HILL

2: EVENLODE VILLAGE CIRCULAR

3: ADLESTROP, ODDINGTON AND DAYLESFORD

4: KINGHAM AND BLEDINGTON HEATH

5: BLEDINGTON AND FOXHOLES

6: SHIPTON, LYNEHAM AND BRUERN

7: SHIPTON AND ASCOTT

8: ASCOTT, SHORTHAMPTON AND CHILSON

9: CHARLBURY, DEAN GROVE AND COLDRON MILL

10: CHARLBURY, CORNBURY AND FAWLER

11: STONESFIELD AND COMBE

12: GLYME VALLEY

13: BLENHEIM PARK

14: LONG HANBOROUGH CIRCULAR

15: AROUND CASSINGTON

The Walks

Walk 1: LONGBOROUGH & BOURTON-ON-THE-HILL

This walk, linking two attractive north Cotswold villages, offers delightful views eastwards over the upper Evenlode valley, enhanced by a backdrop provided by gentle hills of the Oxfordshire Cotswolds.

Longborough, from which the walk begins, stands well on its hillside site, its main street of 17th and 18th century buildings of local stone lying parallel to the Roman Fosse Way, little over a mile distant to the east. Alongside the A424, south-west of the village, are the remains of a Neolithic long barrow, from which the village, first recorded in Domesday Book as Langeberg, may well have taken its name.

St James's church, at the northern end of the village, retains evidence of its Norman origins in the form of doorways in the nave and the corbel table in the chancel. However, its most outstanding feature is its beautiful chantry chapel, dating from the 14th century, when the church belonged to Hailes Abbey, and which contains the effigy of a knight in armour and his lady of the same period. Nearby, and also clad in armour, is the 17th century effigy of Sir William Leigh, together with his wife and children.

The sealed-off north transept contains the tomb of Sir Charles Cockerell of Sezincote (1837), an elaborate affair featuring a bust, angels and heraldry, the work of Sir Richard Westmacott.

Further associations with nearby Sezincote can be seen in the churchyard. These are the graves of the Dugdale family, and include that of F.B. Dugdale, who won the Victoria Cross in the Boer War, only to die in a hunting accident at the age of 25.

An arguable source of the Evenlode: a spring near Bourton

Following the Heart of England Way into Sezincote Park, soon to get our first glimpse of the unique early 19th century house built in the Indian manner, we can readily appreciate why the youthful John Betjeman, invited to spend house-party weekends here by his fellow Oxford undergraduate John Dugdale, revealed in his autobiographical *Summoned by Bells* that these were his happiest days. The Dugdales had arrived at Sezincote from Lancashire in the 1880s, taking over the amazing house, designed by the architect S.P. Cockerell for his brother, newly returned from service with the East India Company. The present house replaced an earlier building, which, like the village of Sezincote, has long since disappeared without trace.

The spacious and beautiful grounds in which the house stands were laid out by Thomas and William Daniell, who had themselves spent much time in India, while the landscaping of the park, making use of the natural contours and streams, was entrusted to the celebrated Humphry Repton.

As its name implies. Bourton-on-the-Hill commands the upper Evenlode valley to the east. A linear village, built from locally quarried stone, it stands astride the main Worcester to London road, which was turnpiked in 1731. Sadly, this steeply-climbing road, now the A44, mars what would otherwise be a most attractive village street—a great pity, as Bourton offers a great deal of interest to the curious visitor.

The church of St Lawrence was a Norman foundation, as can be seen from the two arcade pillars with their carved capitals. However, much of the present building of golden ashlar dates from the 14th century and, complete with fine clerestory and three-stage tower, it stands impressively on its commanding site. Rarely-seen features within the church are the bell-metal standard Winchester bushel and peck, inscribed with the name of the local clerk to the bench of magistrates and dated 1816.

Bourton-on-the–Hill was formerly divided between two manors. Both manor houses survive; that at the top of the village, now known as Manor Farmhouse, stands opposite the Horse and Groom inn and is an 18th century rebuilding. The other manor house, Bourton House, lies below the church and was also rebuilt in the 18th century, having been erected possibly by Richard Palmer, whose initials, together with the date 1570, can be seen on the magnificent tithe barn close by. Richard Palmer was linked by marriage to the Overbury family, one of whom, Sir Thomas, was murdered in the Tower of London in 1613 by the slow administration of poison. He was placed there on the orders of Lady

Bourton church

Essex because he opposed her marriage to Robert Carr, favourite of James I. Together with Bourton House gardens, this building is occasionally open to the public.

Walk 1: LONGBOROUGH to BOURTON ON THE HILL

5 miles (2½ hours). Location: Longborough stands at the junction of 3 unclassified roads, midway between A424 and A429, 2½ miles N of Stow-on-the-Wold. Start: War memorial, Longborough (GR 179297). Park: In village.

A.   From war memorial, pass Coach & Horses inn on left and climb to public footpath along private road on right. At road end, continue along footpath to enter field through gate (Heart of England Way sign). Follow clear path for about ¾ mile to cross estate road and enter park through kissing gate. Aim for waymark on large log. From here, route descends to pass through gateway and on towards woodland. Sezincote House comes into view on left.

Sezincote House

B.   Enter woodland through gate. Cross stream feeding Duckery lake on right (headwater of River Evenlode). Path veers slightly to right. Waymarks on logs indicate route. Pass through woodland strip and over ridge and furrow to stile in fence to left of oak clump. Bourton-on-the-Hill church now visible ahead. Path crosses 2 more fields. At end of second, notice waymark indicating path to right (return route). Keep straight on, passing shallow well ('Deo gratias 1919' inscribed on nearby wall) to enter Bourton-on-the-Hill.

⸱   C   To explore village, turn left up lane and follow it to right to reach main street (A44). Turn right into churchyard, leaving down steps at far corner   to regain lane walked earlier. Turn right to regain outward route. (Bourton House gardens and tithe barn are short way down A44 towards Moreton-in-Marsh). To return to Longborough, retrace steps to waymarked path (now on left) noted earlier. Keep hedge on left over 3 fields. On reaching

point at which hedge swings away to left, turn sharp right between hedges interspersed with oaks. Cross stile and follow path to left, passing new planting. Cross drive over stiles and keep hedge on left to cross footbridge. Go through spinney and leave over stile. Keep hedge on left to cross footbridge at confluence of streams. Path swings to left and keeps hedge on right to join surfaced road. Turn right. Pass 2 cattle grids and farm (Upper Rye Farm) on right to reach cross path.

D Turn left past barn and follow curving track over field to go through gate. Follow woodland edge to right then cross field to reach tree stump indicating crossways of paths. Turn right along Monarch's Way. Go through gate and keep wood on right at first before crossing field to footbridge by oak tree. Go over field to stile. Pinnacles of Longborough church now visible ahead. In next field, aim for left hand corner to cross stile and footbridge by

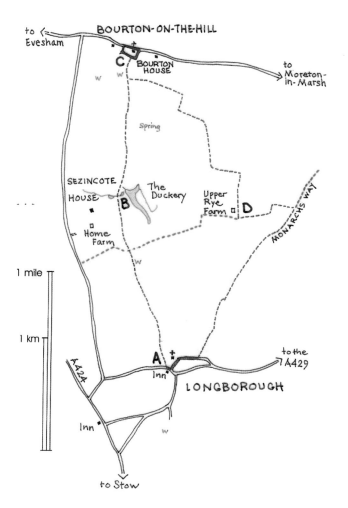

1 mile

1 km

Public transport: Train to Moreton-in-Marsh; then bus to Bourton-on-the-Hill (01905 763888). Walk can be started/finished here.

ash tree. Keep hedge on right up to stile, followed by another on right in 10 yards. Go half left over field to cross stile leading to path between houses. At end, turn right into Longborough. War memorial is to left of church.

Map: O.S. Explorer OL 45 The Cotswolds.

Refreshments: Coach & Horses Inn, Longborough (01451 830325); Horse & Groom, Bourton on the Hill (0386 700413).

Walk 2: EVENLODE VILLAGE CIRCULAR

Evenlode church

evenly along a roughly rectangular grid of lanes, with the church commanding a sharp corner at the western extremity, a mere two hundred yards or so from the river.

Yet despite their close proximity, village and river have been divided from one another since the coming of the railway in the 1850s. In fact, the only access points to the Evenlode from the village are the bridleway crossing the line near Stratford Bridge to the north and Stock Bridge, carrying the road to Broadwell, over a mile distant to the south.

Although walkers determined to trace the upper reaches of the River Evenlode may wish to commence their explorations amidst the modern housing developments on the southernmost fringe of Moreton-in-Marsh, it is not until the rivulet approaches its namesake village that the valley offers pleasant country walking.

Evenlode village, from which this easy, if unspectacular circular ramble begins, and which, as was pointed out in the introduction, gave its name to the river, was one of several detached segments of Worcestershire that were transferred to Gloucestershire in 1931, thus depriving the Four Shires Stone, at the parish's far northern point, of much of its raison d'etre. Deriving its name from the old English 'Eowla's watercourse or river crossing', it is a small village scattered un-

As happened with other lines spreading over the countryside during the years of 'railway mania', the proposal for an Oxford to Worcester line met with formidable resistance from local landowners, in this case the influential Lord Redesdale of Batsford Park, who in a letter to the rector of Kingham, wrote: 'I trust you will oppose by every means in your power, this horrid railway, which will cut up many of our finest meadows.' Knowing that the Rev. Lockwood, like himself, was a keen fox hunter, Redesdale must have confidently expected his wholehearted support, whereas

The Oxford, Worcester and Wolverhampton Railway lives on: mileage marking on bridge

in fact Lockwood did all he could to promote the railway.

Its roughly rectangular layout makes Evenlode an inviting prospect for leisurely exploration, with St Edward's church the obvious starting point. All that remains of the original Norman building is the chancel arch but the 14th century is well represented, with three-stage embattled tower, south aisle and exceptionally fine carved oak pulpit. Traces of wall painting were revealed during the vigorous restoration carried out in the 1880s.

The main village street, along which the walk commences, is essentially Cotswold in character and contains some good examples of farmhouses and associated buildings of varying periods, notably a house with striking Gothic windows at the T-junction. To the right, off the route, lies the village green, with the former school opposite, followed by an alluring lane leading eastwards towards the neighbouring village of Chastleton, famed for

its National Trust property, the early 17th century Chastleton House.

Returning to the route of the walk, users of Ordnance Survey maps of pre-1997 vintage should note that the footpath diversion of that date led to a major re-routing in the vicinity of Coldicote Farm. Instead of passing close to the farm buildings, the route now lies further to the west – a distinct advantage as far as the tracing of the Evenlode is concerned, as the revised route takes the walker alongside the infant river before joining the bridleway to the west of the original point.

The imposing-sounding Stratford Bridge spanning the Evenlode and crossed on the return route, is in fact a modest cart bridge, possibly named after a local farmer. Its position is shown as Stratford's Ford on the original Ordnance Survey map.

15th century pulpit in Evenlode church

Walk 2: EVENLODE VILLAGE CIRCULAR
5 miles (2½ hours). Location: Evenlode lies 2 miles SE of Moreton-in-Marsh. Start: church (GR 221291). Street parking nearby.

A With church on left, walk to road junction and turn left (Moreton-in-Marsh signpost). Follow road for about half a mile, passing Poplars Farm and no-through-road on right to reach bridleway on left. Proceed through 3 gates on to tree-lined path. Path bends to right and, after 200 yards, to left to reach crossways of paths at marker post.

B Turn right over stile alongside gate. Cross field, passing between two trees, to go over stile and footbridge. Continue straight on, over second bridge and across field, leaving through hand-gate, with woodland and reedbed on left. Follow wood side for 50 yards to stile in fence. The path now veers to the left across a narrow field to a gated footbridge. Cross next field to pass through left hand of 2 gates. Keep hedge on right as far as the gate on right. Turn through this and cross field, aiming for far left hand corner. Pass through, or round, 4 kissing-gates and keep on alongside the infant River Evenlode (Moreton-in-Marsh church spire is visible ahead) to reach track.

Four Shires Stone

C Turn left on to track. Cross cart bridge and railway bridge to reach T–junction of tracks. Turn left. The rest of the walk is along part of the Diamond Way, a long-distance walk created to commemorate the 60th anniversry of the founding of the Ramblers' Association.

Cross another arm of the Evenlode, this time coming from the Sezincote direction, and go through metal gate. Cross field, aiming for the barns of Frogmore Farm, approached over 2 stiles. Cross a third stile by the barn. Path skirts to left of barns to cross farm road and continues straight on along field edge with hedge on right. About 100 yards from field end pass through large gap in hedge and continue with hedge (and ditch) on left. Pass wood on left to continue with hedge on left to reach waymarked crossing track.

D Turn left, with hedge on left for one field-length, then cross next field to reach the river. Cross Evenlode over Stratford Bridge and continue over railway at 90-mile post (Care!). Cross narrow field with new plantation on left; go through gate and continue up wooded path to rejoin outward route by marker post at cross-ways (B).

Turn right. Cross field along line indicated by waymark to reach and follow grassy track climbing towards long metal barn. Pass to right of barn. Cross stile straight ahead and continue, with hedge on right. At bend in hedge, look out for double stile on right. Cross this and the corner of the next field to a final stile, giving access to drive. Turn left to reach road, then right to retrace steps into Evenlode village and back to the start.

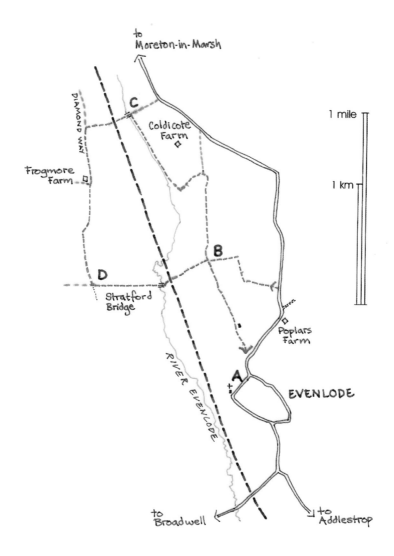

Map: O.S. Explorer OL 45 The Cotswolds.
Refreshments: Nearest at Broadwell (Fox Inn) and Moreton-in-Marsh.

Walk 3: ADLESTROP, ODDINGTON & DAYLESFORD

Adlestrop remembered

Although short, this walk takes in three interesting yet contrasting villages, each of which has its own special claim to fame. Adlestrop, from which the walk begins, is arguably the best-known Cotswold village of all, not as a tripper destination—Bourton-on-the-Water lays claim to that dubious distinction—but on account of the much-anthologised poem by Edward Thomas, which to countless admirers has come to represent the quintessential English countryside as it was in the distant days of steam.

Indeed, the association between Thomas and Adlestrop, though confined to a sixteen-line poem composed after his express train 'drew up unwontedly' one day in June 1914, prompted Anne Harvey to gather sufficient material—'all that seems curious, relevant,

coincidental and intriguing'—to compile a whole book on the subject (*Adlestrop Revisited*. Sutton Publishing.1999). And although there is no evidence that Thomas ever set foot in the village, one of the Great Western name boards, saved when the station was closed in the 1960s; a plaque bearing the poem on a platform seat; and a mural in the village hall ensure that his memory here remains forever green.

Jane Austen, by contrast, is known to have visited Adlestrop on at least three occasions, staying with her uncle, the rector, the Rev. Thomas Leigh at the Rectory, later known as Adlestrop House, and situated opposite the church of St Mary Magdalene. During these visits, which took place between 1794 and 1806, Jane spent some time in the newly-created grounds and gardens of nearby Adlestrop Park, home of another relative, James Henry Leigh. Students of Austen's work are of the opinion that the fictitious village of Thornton Lacey in Mansfield Park (1814) is in fact based on Adlestrop.

Oddington, the largest by far of the trio

of villages visited on the walk, is divided into two parts, Upper and Lower. It is the latter that features on the route and in which stands one of the most appealing churches in the entire Cotswolds. Situated along a lane to the south of the village, the Norman church of St Nicholas is all that remains of the original Saxon settlement of Otintone, on which old Oddington stood until the early 18th century. By this time, most of the villagers had moved uphill and when, in 1852, a new church was built on the higher ground, the old building was virtually abandoned—so much so that a vixen is said to have reared her cubs in the beautiful Jacobean pulpit.

It was not until the arrival of a new rector in 1912 that work began to restore the ancient church. This lengthy and painstaking process finally ensured that such treasures as the awe-inspiring Doom wall painting were preserved for all to see.

After crossing the Evenlode and the railway, two buildings come into view away to the left. Daylesford rectory was the birthplace in 1888 of Frederick (Freddy) Grisewood, the popular radio personality, his father being rector of the little church alongside. In his autobiography, *The World Goes By* (1952), Grisewood recalls spending an idyllic boyhood by the river: 'The Evenlode laid a magic spell on us, and we spent the greater part of our holidays in, on and around it……..(it) ran past two of my father's fields, and that was a never-failing source of mystery and adventure; water-rats to hunt, tiddlers to be caught, and there was too the glorious possibility of a trout.' Crayfish, too were abundant and Grisewood went on to describe how he and his friends 'used to get up properly organised 'crayfish parties', and set nets for them. We'd put the nets down with all sorts of indescribable bait on them in the afternoon and then sally forth with lanterns in the evening and pick them and the feeding crayfish up.'

Daylesford is best known for its associations with Warren Hastings, Governor General of the East India Company, who built Daylesford House, and whose grave, marked by a neo-Greek monument, can be seen in the churchyard.

Evenlode crayfish enjoying their last meal

Walk 3: ADLESTROP, ODDINGTON & DAYLESFORD
3 ¾ miles (2 hours). Location: Adlestrop lies off A436, 3 miles E of Stow-on-the-Wold. Start: Village hall car park (GR 242272).

A   On leaving car park, turn right. Cross stile on left at point where farm drive joins road. Cross field diagonally to footbridge over stream. Follow left hand field margin to reach road. Turn left. At T-junction with A436, turn right along pavement. Beyond bridge spanning railway and Evenlode, cross to left hand verge and follow it to left turn, signposted Lower Oddington.

B   Walk into village. Fox Inn on right at bend. Beyond, take first turn on left just before post box, along lane signposted St Nicholas' church. Beyond church, continue straight on along bridleway. Pass public footpath signposted on left. Continue as far as bridleway sign, also on left.

C   Follow gravel track across field to meeting of two hedges. Continue along same line, with hedge on right. Path eventually veers to right after two trees to cross ditch and go over small field to footbridge over Evenlode. Cross another field to gateway and climb over railway bridge. Keep hedge on left to reach road.

D   Turn left into Daylesford. Church is on left. Continue along lane to T-junction. Go straight aross A436 to pass lodge (no waymark). Follow drive. Path swings to right along edge of cricket field to enter lane through gate. Climb to Adlestrop. Pass church on right. Keep left at fork by the Post Office and descend past cottages back to car park.

Adlestrop Station in the 1920s

22

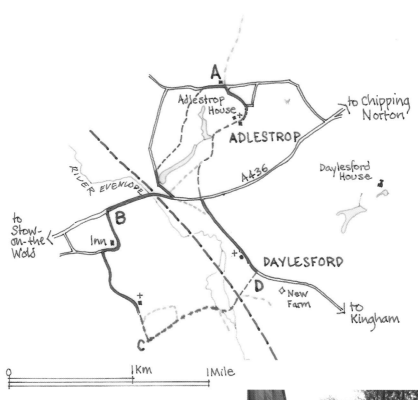

Map: O.S. Explorer OL 45 The Cotswolds.
Refreshments: Fox Inn, Lower Oddington (01451 870555); Daylesford Organic Farm Shop (01608 731700); Adlestrop Post Office(01608 659475).

Warren Hastings' memorial

23

Walk 4: KINGHAM & BLEDINGTON HEATH

Beyond Daylesford, the River Evenlode forms the county boundary between Gloucestershire and Oxfordshire and the route of this walk extends northwards from Kingham to link up with Walk 3 at the railway bridge crossed on that walk.

The water meadows along this stretch of the Evenlode valley are prone to flooding and the walk is best undertaken during a spell of dry weather. Even then, the short length of bridleway over Bledington Heath on the return section can be very muddy. There is no indication of this problem on the first stage of the walk, however, which after leaving Kingham consists of a long, straight and somewhat featureless bridleway, from which wide views towards Icomb and Stow-on-the-Wold westwards and of Kingham Hill to the east help to relieve the monotony.

More often than not omitted or at best briefly dismissed by most guide books, Kingham is a village that rewards patient exploration. Built around a roughly triangular pattern of streets, it contains a number of houses displaying alternating bands of grey and tawny-brown limestone, together with garden walls consisting of stone slabs, resembling large roofing slates, held in place by iron ties. There is a spacious green at the northern end of the village, while the southern corner, from which the walk begins, is especially appealing, with handsome cottages, the church, and the former late 17th century rectory, described by Pevsner as 'One of the finest small houses of this date in the county'.

Kingham Station layout, ca 1920

Ironically, it is for its railway station, rather than for its attractiveness as a village that Kingham is best known. Originally known as Chipping Norton Junction, it became even more stategically placed when the branch line was extended to form the cross-country route from Banbury to Cheltenham. The traces of the latter line can still be seen.

It was the railway that in 1869 brought a visitor to Kingham who was later to describe it in loving yet scholarly prose reminiscent of Gilbert White's writings on Selborne. William Warde Fowler, an Oxford don and prolific author on the Roman civilisation, was to reside in the village for almost fifty years, pursuing his hobby of ornithology and writing a minor classic, *Kingham Old and New*. In this book, published in 1913, together with his earlier *A Year with the Birds*, Fowler wrote engagingly about his rambles in and around the Evenlode valley and in so doing provides the modern reader with a valuable insight into the natural history of the region during the early 20th century.

Two Kingham water meadows in particular provided happy hunting grounds for Fowler. One, the Yantle, or Yantell, lies alongside a tributary of the Evenlode, the Swailsford Brook, flowing from the direction of Chipping Norton. Fowler recorded vast flocks of lapwings in this field, as well as great numbers of winter-visiting redwings and fieldfares. The occasional gull visited the meadow in times of flood and one March day Fowler was delighted to discover four curlews, presumably breaking their journey to their breeding grounds.

Great was Fowler's indignation on one of his visits to the Yantle to find the brook polluted by dye that had been discharged from Bliss Mill, the Chipping Norton tweed mill. His letter of complaint was swiftly acted upon but not before a great number of fish had been poisoned.

Even dearer than the Yantle to Fowler was a meadow known as Coxmoor, to which he devotes a whole chapter in *Kingham Old and New*, beginning: 'There is a certain meadow, long and narrow, with the railway at its northern and the Evenlode as its southern boundary, through which a well used footpath leads to Bledington, crossing the brook by a wooden bridge the wettest end of it is planted

William Warde Fowler with Lummy

with osiers, which greatly add to the attractiveness of the spot both for birds and plants and even for human beings. The footpath to Bledington, after crossing the railway, drops down into the flat just at the corner of this osier bed, and then skirts it till it reaches the brook and the bridge.'

Ninety or so years later, it is reassuring to find that although our route is the reverse of that described by Fowler, it remains instantly recognisable today. True, the osier bed, in which he observed a small colony of marsh warblers over a number of years, has been long since overgrown but having read Fowler's enthusiastic account of the variety of wild life encountered in this corner of Coxmoor, it is impossible to pass this way without experiencing a sense of anticipation.

Walk 4: KINGHAM & BLEDINGTON HEATH

4½ miles (2½ hours). Short option: 3 ¼ miles (2 hours). Location: Kingham lies off B4450, 4 miles SW of Chipping Norton. Start: Church (GR 259238). Street parking.

A   From church, walk into village. Take first turn on left (Cozens Lane). At end, turn left, then right at fork by lime tree. Road soon becomes track (bridleway). Daylesford church spire visible in distance

Short option: Approaching barns, turn off left along field edge (no waymark) and follow it to right to cross railway bridge .Continue to cross Evenlode and join main route at C. Turn left along it.

To follow main route, continue past barns with hedge on right. Pass extensive farm buildings away to right. Beyond these, route veers to left to cross railway bridge. Descend bank, pass through gate and continue over field to cross bridge spanning Evenlode

B   Turn left along river bank. Extensive woodland (Lower Oddington Ashes) lies to right. Approaching woodland limit, ignore path on right. Instead, proceed for about 100 yards beyond woodland to reach waymark on tree stump in gap in hedge. Cross field corner to footbridge and follow line indicated by waymark across field, aiming for left hand corner of woodland. Swing right along woodland edge to reach bridleway,over stile. Turn left and continue to reach cross-path (bridleway to left, footpath to right).

C   Continue straight on for short distance to reach stile on left leading to riverside footpath. Path is clearly waymarked as far as next river crossing. However, short detours may be needed to avoid patches of standing water.

Kingham church tower on left provides guide to distance still to cover.

D   Cross Evenlode over footbridge to re-enter Oxfordshire. Clear path skirts Coxmoor and passes old osier bed on right to reach stile. Path now parallel to railway as far as gated crossing. From her a clear track leads to road, with Kingham church ahead, reached from beyond bus shelter by path over field which avoids dangerous corner.

Kingham rectory

26

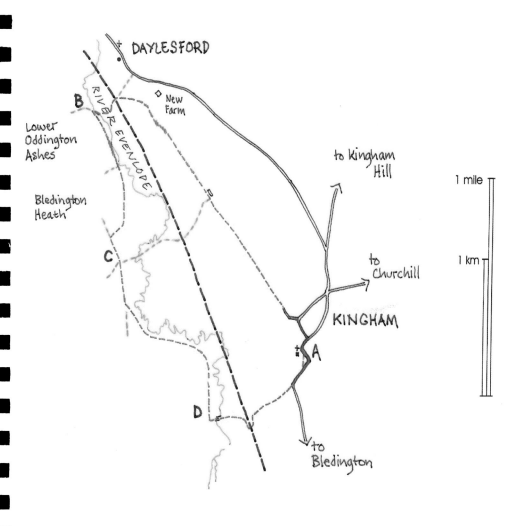

Public transport: Train to Kingham; then Rail-Link bus (01865 772250) to Kingham village.
Map: O.S. Explorer OL 45 The Cotswolds.

Refreshments: Plough Inn (01608 658327) and Mill House Hotel (01608 658188), Kingham. King's Head, Bledington (01608 658365).

Walk 5: BLEDINGTON & FOXHOLES

Bledington Mill

Separated from Oxfordshire by the Evenlode and the southernmost Gloucestershire village on the river, Bledington is so called from the original name for the Evenlode and appears as Bladintyn in Domesday Book (i.e. Farmstead on the River Bladen).

It is quite a large village by Evenlode valley standards, with the older part, which contains several elegant houses of Cotswold stone grouped around an extensive green, through which a tributary stream of the Evenlode picks its way. This stream is the domain of the local ducks, which when not dabbling are inclined to squat down in the middle of the road – hence the warning sign to motorists at the approach to the green.

It comes as something of a surprise to discover a rash of red brick elsewhere in the village, a reminder that there was once a small brickworks here. This intrusion may well have influenced Herbert Evans, who on cycling through Bledington in 1908, collecting material for his book *Highways and Byways in Oxford and the Cotswolds*, considered it to have 'the deserted melancholy air of one which has seen better days.'

However, in common with other writers who seek out St Leonard's church at the south-western edge of the village, Evans was quick to concede that here was a building of exceptional quality. For this 12th century church, with its 15th century additions of tower, raised nave and noble perpendicular windows filled with beautiful stained glass, ranks among the finest in east Gloucestershire. At the time of its enlargement, in the 15th century, it belonged to Winchcombe Abbey, and the quality of workmanship gives some idea of the wealth then generated by the thriving wool trade, in which successive abbots were prominent figures.

Another association with Winchcombe Abbey can be seen midway between the church and the green. This is the 17th century Manor Farm, which stands on the site of a rest-house for the monks of the abbey.

Before leaving Bledington, the walk passes a former water mill, the first encountered on the Evenlode. This stands by the B4450, not far from Kingham station and two of the grinding stones can be seen against the wall. It ceased working in the 1930s. A mill was recorded in Domesday Book, valued at five shillings, and may well have stood at this spot.

Morris dancing was traditionally associated with Bledington and as late as 1913, Cecil Sharp visited the village to interview two local elderly men, the fiddler Charles Benfield and Edwin Gibbs, both of whom had formerly been part of the Bledington team, noted for their own special dance, the Bledington Hey Away.

Beyond Bledington, the route follows a length of the Oxfordshire Way long-distance footpath, established in 1976 and extending from Bourton-on-the-Water to Henley-on-Thames. This leads to Foxholes Farm , where it links up once more with the Evenlode before swinging to the south-west to enter Foxholes Nature Reserve, administered by the Berks, Bucks and Oxon Wildlife Trust.

Known locally as Bould Wood, from the nearby hamlet of that name, the reserve is a remnant of the ancient royal hunting forest of Wychwood. It contains a variety of habitats, ranging from oak and ash woodland to wet meadow. Spring flowers present include primrose, early purple orchid and twayblade, while fungi abound in autumn. Several species of butterflies are on the wing during late spring and summer and breeding birds include great, coal and blue tit, nuthatch, treecreeper, great-spotted woodpecker and sparrowhawk

Leaving the woodland at the approach to Bould, the walk continues along a minor road as far as the next hamlet, Foscot, from which a footpath crosses fields to reach a bridge over the Westcote Brook, a substantial tributary of the Evenlode, flowing from its source near the escarpment dividing the Windrush and Evenlode valleys to join the latter river near Bledington mill.

A gentle climb follows to reach another section of the Oxfordshire Way, which leads via Bledington church back to the start.

Walk 5: BLEDINGTON & FOXHOLES

4 miles (2 hours). Location: Bledington lies on B4450, 4 miles SE of Stow on-the-Wold. Start: Village green (GR 244228). Street parking.

A   From village green, walk away from King's Arms to bend by village stores. Cross straight over along Chapel Lane (no through road). Lane eventually veers to right and narrows before becoming track leading into field. Follow left hand edge, passing (NOT crossing) footbridge. Continue along stream to meet Evenlode. Cross stile and follow narrow path between hedge and wire fence. At end, follow field edge to cross 2 stiles and reach B4450 at former mill. Turn right along pavement to reach junction.

B   Follow Foscot – Idbury sign to left. Cross Westcote Brook and turn left at Oxfordshire Way sign. Follow public bridleway signs (blue arrows) through gates and to right along clear path. On reaching woodland, path veers to right. At woodland limit, follow waymark to left as far as concrete bridge. Instead of crossing, turn right along stream to reach meeting of paths at bridge.

C   Turn right to enter woodland. Continue straight on to join roughly-surfaced track leading to farm buildings (Foxholes). Keep straight on, passing houses on left to enter field through gate. Leave by second gate to enter nature reserve. Follow bridleway as far as kissing-gate on right alongside marker post. (This gate leads to winding woodland path parallel to wet bridleway). On joining bridleway, turn right along it and follow its winding course through Bould Wood. On leaving wood, bridleway follows left hand field edge to meet road at hamlet of Bould.

D   Turn right along road and continue as far as stile {no waymark} on left just before Foscot sign. Cross field corner to pass through 2 gates in hedge. Go over ridge and furrow and cross Westcote Brook by footbridge. Go over stile and cross field to follow hedge on right. Clear path climbs to join Oxfordshire Way. Turn right to pass through burial ground and pass church to reach bend in road. Turn left back to village green.

Bledington Green

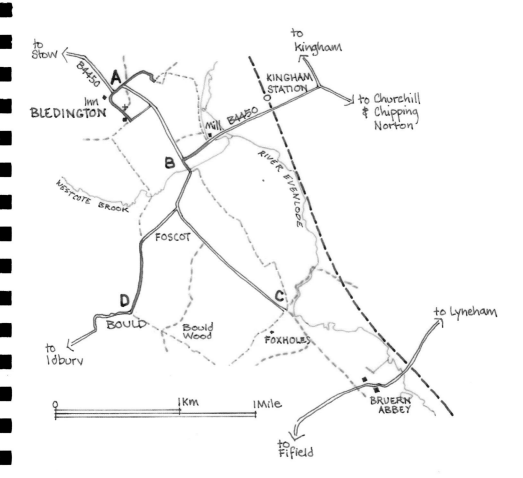

Public Transport: Train to Kingham, then Rail-Link bus (01865 772250) to Bledington Green Map: O.S. Explorer OL 45 The Cotswolds. Refreshments: King's Head, Bledington (01608 658365).

Foxholes

Walk 6: SHIPTON, LYNEHAM & BRUERN

The first of two walks along the Evenlode valley from Shipton-under-Wychwood, this easy circular ramble links up with Walk 5 at Foxholes. Never more than half a mile from the river and the railway which keeps it company, its route traverses quiet, open country for the most part, with only one small settlement, Lyneham, together with its golf course, encountered along the way.

Shipton Church

Shipton is the largest of the three Wychwood villages and despite its situation on the A361 Burford – Chipping Norton road, it manages to retain a distinct village character, with a happy blend of traditional Cotswold buildings and tasteful modern developments. The area around the spacious village green is especially pleasing. Fronting it is the Shaven Crown inn, which dates from the 15th century, having been built as a hostelry for nearby Bruern Abbey. Many original architectural features, including central hall, archway, mullioned windows and paved courtyard have survived the centuries.

Across the road, at the top of the green, stands a monument, in the form of a drinking fountain, to 17 villagers who lost their lives when the steamship Cospatrick, on which they were emigrating to New Zealand, caught fire off Tristan da Cunha in 1874.

St Mary's church, at the foot of the green, dates from the 13th century and contains work from the 14th and 15th centuries, including a fine stone pulpit and an octagonal font decorated with a carving of the bear and ragged staff, the badge of the influential Beauchamps. The table of rectors includes the name of John Foxe, who is said to have written his *Book of Martyrs* during his ministry here (1563-1587).

In the churchyard can be seen a unique three-deck bale-top tomb, dating from 1734 and marking the grave of the Morgan family. Behind the church, close to the bank of the Evenlode, stands the elegant Prebendal House, built by Christ Church, Oxford, and dating from the early 16th century.

Beyond Standbow Bridge, the northern-most limit of the walk, the route follows the riverbank for a short distance, thus providing an all-too-rare opportunity to observe the flora and fauna of what is by now a sizable river. Sadly, the once abundant water vole is no longer a familiar sight along the Evenlode but vigilant walkers may be fortunate enough to catch a fleeting glimpse of a kingfisher streaking low over the water.

At Lyneham, the route follows a short section of the D'Arcy Dalton Way. Opened in 1987, this 65-mile footpath extends from Wormleigh Reservoir, north of Banbury, to Wayland's Smithy, on the Ridgeway

On linking up with Walk 5 at Foxholes, the route heads in a south easterly direction, following the Oxfordshire Way through Cocksmoor

Wood, the first part of which, together with the wet meadow extending down to the Evenlode, forms the eastern extremity of the Foxholes Nature Reserve. Mud can be expected through the wood after rain but the damp conditions favour a range of flowering plants, mosses and liverworts. As on Walk 5, woodland bird life provides plenty of interest.

After crossing a road, the elegant pile of Bruern Abbey comes into view. The name is deceptive; there was indeed an abbey here – built by the Cistercians in 1137 – but no trace remains. The present building dates from about 1720 but was partly rebuilt following a fire in 1780. Further alteration took place in the 1970s. It has served as a school and as a private residence in recent times.

Bruern Abbey

Walk 6: SHIPTON, LYNEHAM & BRUERN

5½ miles (3 hours). Location: Shipton-under-Wychwood. The village stands on the A361, 4 miles NE of Burford. Start: Village green (GR 280180). Street parking.

Cospatrick Memorial

A　From lane alongside village green, walk towards church. Immediately before churchyard, turn left along footpath and follow it to reach A361. Turn right and then first left along Meadow Lane. Beyond houses, lane continues as track. When Oxfordshire Way swings to left, keep straight on to cross Evenlode and pass under railway .Route now follows right hand fringe of recently-planted woodland to cross footbridge and enter large field. Follow line indicated by waymark across field to reach hedge. Turn left along it and continue through gateway. In 30 yards, at marker post, cross ridge and furrow to right to reach road opposite farm buildings.

B　Turn right. Pass Priory Farm and turn left into Lyneham. At right hand bend, continue straight on (D'Arcy Dalton Way signpost). Continue along track by side of golf course. Cross stile by cottage and keep straight on along track with golf course on both sides to reach road through gap in hedge. Cross straight over and across field. Path passes between woods and across another field to reach railway via two gates. Cross with care to enter field over stile. Go diagonally across field to cross stream (Sars Brook) by bridge with handrails, and continue to bridle track coming from railway bridge. Turn left on to bridle track, which leads to the bank of the Evenlode at Standbow bridge. Cross bridge and turn left along bank of river. Follow as far as cart bridge over stream at meeting of paths.

C　Follow path straight ahead up slope and into gap in trees to join Oxfordshire Way (bridleway – blue arrow). Turn left along it. The Way passes through the wood at first, then along woodland edge before crossing road at Bruern. Pass Abbey on left. Route continues over fields and between woods. Beyond well-sited memorial seat, route passes through gates to cross road, maintaining direct course towards Shipton church spire before swinging to left at hedge corner.

D　Follow hedge down to join outward route. Turn right along it to reach Meadow Lane. Retrace steps back to start.

The Evenlode near Standbow Bridge

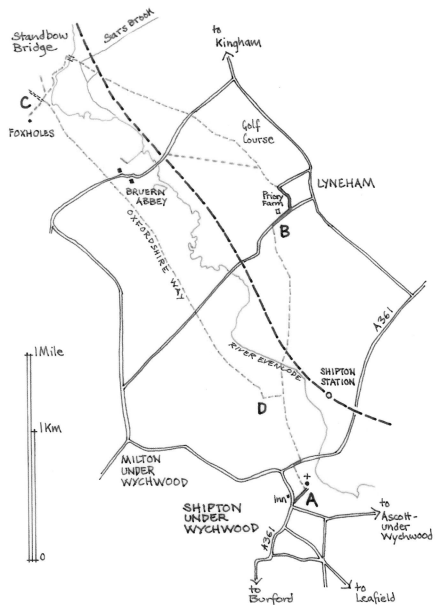

Standbow Bridge

Sars Brook

to Kingham

C

FOXHOLES

Golf Course

LYNEHAM

BRUERN ABBEY

OXFORDSHIRE WAY

Priory Farm

B

A 361

1 Mile

1 Km

RIVER EVENLODE

SHIPTON STATION

D

0

MILTON UNDER WYCHWOOD

Inn

A

SHIPTON UNDER WYCHWOOD

A 361

to Ascott-under-Wychwood

to Burford

to Leafield

Public transport: Train to Shipton (infrequent) or to Charlbury, then Rail-Link bus (01608 677322) to Shipton. Map: O.S. Explorer OL 45 The Cotswolds.
Refreshments: Lamb Inn (01993 830465), Red Horse (01993 830391) and Shaven Crown (01993 830330), all Shipton-under-Wychwood; Kiosk (Halfway House) on golf course.

Walk 7: SHIPTON & ASCOTT

Motte and Bailey vestiges, Ascott Earl

The start of this second circular walk along the Evenlode valley from Shipton-under-Wychwood entails covering a short length of the beginning of Walk 6 before crossing the river and striking off eastwards along field paths between river and railway towards Ascott-under-Wychwood. The route keeps to the riverside for a short stretch before deviating near the point at which the mill steam branches off to Langley mill, after which it merges with the Oxfordshire Way before crossing the Evenlode once more at the approach to Ascott.

Ascott-under-Wychwood is made up of two ancient settlements, each with a castle site. Ascott d'Oyley is seen on Walk 8, while Ascott Earl comprises the southern half of the village. The motte and bailey castle once stood on the gently rising ground overlooking the Evenlode and its site, now merely grassy mounds, can be seen away to the left,

backed by houses, on entering Ascott.

Present day Ascott consists of a long village street with the 12th century church of Holy Trinity, set in a spacious churchyard featuring lines of lime trees, standing in a commanding position midway between the two castle sites. The scene is a peaceful one today but this was far from the case in May 1873, when after members of the newly-formed farm labourers' union went on strike in protest at the dismissal of a carter, their

Sheepwash, Ascott

employer, an Ascott farmer, locked out his men and brought in non-union labour from elsewhere. At this, a group of labourers' wives, later known as 'The Ascott Martyrs', armed themselves with sticks and confronted the strike breakers. Although no force was in fact used, the women were arrested and local magistrates sentenced them to prison with hard labour. This injustice caused widespread protest, which prompted their eventual release amid public celebration. It was generally agreed that the national publicity that stemmed from the women's action played a significant part in ensuring an improvement in the lot of farmworkers during the time of the agricultural depression. Memorial plaques on seats around a tree on the triangular green north of the church commemorate the women's stand.

Leaving Ascott, the route follows a public footpath southwards alongside the delightful Coldwell Brook, passing a recently restored sheepwash and fishpond before reaching the B4437.

Back at Shipton, the route passes through the pleasant southern extremity of the village before climbing to reach the A361. A short distance along on the right stands Shipton Court, a magnificent early Jacobean house attributed to the Lacy family and dating from 1603. The beautifully proportioned west front, facing the road, consists of eleven bays, with five narrow gables. Alongside, a massive wall and former stabling are equally impressive, as is a four-gabled dovecote nearby. An elegant lime avenue lies opposite.

Shipton Court

37

Walk 7: SHIPTON & ASCOTT

4¾ miles (2½ hours). Location: Shipton under Wychwood. The village stands on the A361, 4 miles NE of Burford. Start: Village green (GR 280180). Street parking.

A   From lane alongside village green, walk towards church. Immediately before churchyard, turn left along footpath and follow it to reach A361. Turn right along pavement. Cross Evenlode and continue to reach footpath sign on right immediately beyond garage. Go through handgate and follow direction indicated by left hand waymark over field to cross stile behind remains of building. Turn right along field edge. Path eventually keeps Evenlode on right. Cross stile, followed by footbridge over stream. Route now follows wide path between trees to join Oxfordshire Way, coming in from left. Beyond gate, continue along hedged track to cross Evenlode (remains of motte and bailey visible on left from bridge) and reach Ascott Earl.

B   To see Ascott under Wychwood, turn left along village street. Turn right in front of church and right again along Heritage Lane. This continues as footpath leading to road between houses, leading in turn back to village street. Retrace left back to Ascott Earl. Follow road round to left. Soon, at right hand bend, turn left at footpath sign along gated track, passing restored sheepwash and former fishpond. Beyond farm buildings, route becomes footpath with stiles along brookside to cross footbridge and reach B4437.

C   Turn right along verge and continue for about half mile. At left hand bend, follow footpath sign on right. Cross stile and keep fence on right to reach waymark. Turn left here along bank. Cross stile and follow clear path to reach road close by Shipton sign. Cross straight over along footpath to reach another road

D   Turn left, then immediately right along track through allotments. At its end, turn right, then left, down to lane. Turn right and follow lane, which dips before climbing to pass converted chapel and reach T-junction. Turn right to pass Lamb inn and reach A361. Follow this to right into Shipton, passing Court on right to reach village green and start.

The Evenlode Valley near Ascott: gentle and lush.

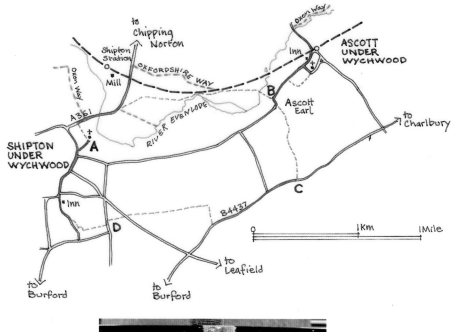

Martyrs plaque, Ascott-under-Wychwood

Public transport: Train to Shipton (infrequent) or to Charlbury, then Rail-Link bus (01608 677322) to Shipton). Maps: OS Explorer180 Oxford Witney and Woodstock/O.S. Explorer OL 45 The Cotswolds.

Refreshments: Swan Inn, Ascott-under-Wychwood (01993 830345); Lamb Inn (01993 830465), Red Horse (01993 830391) and Shaven Crown (01993 830330), all Shipton-under-Wychwood.

Walk 8: ASCOTT, SHORTHAMPTON & CHILSON

Pudlicote House

This walk commences at the northern end of Ascott-under-Wychwood, known formerly as Ascott d'Oyley. Less than a mile separates this settlement from Ascott Earl, visited on the previous walk and like its southern neighbour, it retains a vestige of the castle that once dominated this part of the Evenlode valley.

Taking its name from the family of the Norman, Wido de Oileio, who accompanied the invading William the Conqueror, the castle, now a series of humps and hollows adjacent to the later manor house, dates from about 1130. Like many other castles built at the time, it appears to have had a short life, although excavations carried out in the 1940s revealed an extensive stone tower and evidence of later buildings.

On the same site is the 16th century manor house, together with a substantial old barn and a timber-framed granary on staddle stones

A short distance along the Oxfordshire Way is all that remains of Pudlicote ('The cottage by the puddle' (stream). This small village stood on land belonging to Eynsham Abbey and was deserted by the mid 14th century. The present Pudlicote House was built in 1810 and the parkland in which it stands, with its noble oaks, dates from that time. Happily, the name of Pudlicote is perpetuated in Charlbury parish church, in which can be seen an aisle bearing the name.

Shorthampton church

George (15th century)–as well as a Tudor window and 18th century box pews

A lonely bridleway, with Wychwood Forest dominating the southern horizon and the broad sweep of the Evenlode valley drawing the eye northwards, leads to another attractive hamlet, Chilson. This unusual name is derived from the Old English and is said to have indicated the dwelling of a young nobleman. Nobility may have long since departed but the place has an orderly yet comfortable feel to it, with its former modest cottages, barns and little school all converted into pleasant modern homes.

Leaving Chilson behind, the route descends gently, on a parallel course to the Charlbury-Burford high road, before swinging abruptly westwards towards Ascott-under-Wychwood, reached at Mill Lane, by Yew Tree Farm. The lane continues as High Street, along which a number of old and attractive stone houses line the route back to the start.

Ample compensation for leaving the riverside footpath at Catsham Bridge is provided by the diversion to Shorthampton, reached after a gentle climb above the valley. Tiny and remote are words that come readily to mind, describing as they do both the hamlet itself and All Saints' church, although Dr Nikolaus Pevsner, in his book on Oxfordshire in the *Buildings of England* series, preferred 'small and humble' to describe the latter.

There can be no disputing the charm of this church, which retains several of its original 12th century features, while at the same time displaying later additions – wall paintings, discovered in 1903, depicting amongst others St Leonard and St Frideswide (14th century) and St Zita and St

Chilson

Walk 8: ASCOTT, SHORTHAMPTON & CHILSON

5¾ miles (3 hours). Location: Ascott under Wychwood. The village lies 5 miles NE of Burford. Start: Village green (GR 302187). Street parking.

A   From green, take Chipping Norton road over level crossing to reach private drive (public footpath) on right, leading to Manor Farm. Route swings to left opposite buildings. Grassy track leads to bridge over Evenlode. Beyond bridge, route keeps first river, then hedge on right, to gate. Beyond, route swings to right (blue waymark) and follows field boundary round to stile on line of original route (although most walkers continue straight ahead). In next field, pass remains of barn to stile and continue to pass through parkland with Pudlicote House away to left.

B   Cross Pudlicote Lane. Clear gated path leads to Catsham Lane. Turn right. Cross Evenlode over Catsham Bridge and continue to reach footpath to Shorthampton signposted on right immediately beyond railway bridge.

Path keeps hedge on right for 100 yards. At waymark, cross field, aiming for Shorthampton church. Pass through gateway at top left hand corner of field and follow wall on left to cross stile into lane.

C   To visit church, turn left up lane. To continue walk, either turn right on leaving churchyard and right again along top lane or turn left and follow lane past farm and uphill to reach top lane. Route to Chilson continues as bridleway on same line as top lane.

D   On reaching hamlet of Chilson, turn left along street and continue as far as School Lane on right. At lane end, go through field gate. Route follows margins over 2 fields, then in third field dips to corner and turns to right along boundary. At field end, follow hedge to right for 20 yards to gap. Cross field diagonally

The Evenlode from Catsham Bridge

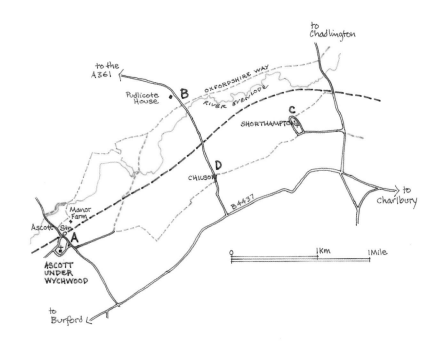

left to reach Mill lane at Ascott D'Oyley. Turn left along lane, which continues as High Street. At end, turn right back to green and start.

Granary on staddle stones

Public transport: Train to Ascott-under-Wychwood (infrequent) or to Charlbury; then Rail-Link bus(01608 677322) to Ascott-under-Wychwood .

Maps: O.S. Explorer 180 Oxford Witney and Woodstock/Outdoor leisure 191 Banbury, Bicester & Chipping Norton.

Refreshments: Swan Inn, Ascott (01993 830345).

Walk 9: CHARLBURY, DEAN GROVE & COLDRON MILL

The little town of Charlbury, perched high above the east bank of the Evenlode, is the only place of any size encountered along the valley. In its day a busy town, the populace largely employed in glove-making, it now thrives as an attractive place to live, with commuting to Oxford or London an easy option by dint of its surprisingly good train service.

The Evenlode in winter, ca 1914

Part of this short walk, the first of two circular rambles from the town, follows the course of the Oxfordshire Way through de-lightful countryside to the north west of Charlbury. The walker is treated to appealing views south across the valley, including the remains of the ancient settlement of Walcot, where once stood the great house of the Jenkinsons, one of whom, Robert, Earl of Liverpool, was Prime Minister during and after the Napoleonic war. Beyond, a swathe of Wychwood Forest, a constant and commanding feature of this stretch of the Evenlode valley, crowns the scene.

A rich diversity of wildlife enriches the walk. Old species-rich hedges and patches of scrub and gorse provide ideal habitat for farmland birds and insects, as well as a colourful array of spring and summer wild

The Campbell memorial

flowers. Dean Grove, an extensive tract of ancient woodland, is especially rewarding, the footpath passing between stands of old oaks and long-abandoned hazel coppice on the way to Coldron Mill.

The former mill, at the confluence of two of the Evenlode's tributaries, the Coldron and Taston brooks, has been converted, as have so many

Living willow fence, Coldron Mill

water mills, into a distinctive private residence, and stands in attractive grounds, edged by a willow fence, with an alluring mill pond close by.

Back at the start of the walk, at the foot of Pound Hill, walkers with time and energy to spare may wish to take another, shorter walk through the Evenlode water meadows (Mill Field), as described at the foot of the route direction page. This stroll was a favourite of W.D. (Bill) Campbell, the locally-born teacher and naturalist, whose books on birds and nature diaries, published in national and local newspapers, won him a wide and devoted readership. A stone in his memory can be seen in the water meadows

Two of Charlbury's oldest buildings, Armada Cottage and Old Talbot, dating from the late 16th century, are passed on Thames Street, the continuation of Pound Hill.

Beating the bounds 1924: the western river crossing

45

Walk 9: CHARLBURY, DEAN GROVE & COLDRON MILL
2¼ miles (1½ hours). Location: Charlbury. Start: small fenced green on left at foot of Pound Hill on B4026 (GR 354199). Roadside parking.

A   From green, follow right-of-way sign along track. At right hand bend, note kissing gate on left (optional riverside walk – see below). At left hand bend, leave track and go through kissing gate. Path keeps hedge on right. Beyond next kissing gate, skirt wood on right to another kissing gate. Now keep fenced-off gorse patch on right. At fence end, keep straight on over field and through woodland belt to cross footbridge and pass through kissing gate into field. At fork, follow right hand waymark to kissing gate in hedge. Cross field to enter Dean Grove through kissing gate.

B   At next waymark, go right through kissing gate. Cross narrow field and go over plank bridge to enter grounds of Coldron Mill.

C   Follow willow fence round to right, then keep left to cross plank bridge with mill pond on left. Climb bank and follow field edge to left. At hedge corner, keep straight on across field to kissing gate. Continue straight on, passing hollow on left to kissing gate. Now keep hedge on left before continuing over field and through woodland to follow hedge on left to kissing gate. Beyond, go

through handgate on right and follow line indicated by waymark, crossing ditch to reach footbridge. Cross this and descend over large field to kissing gate leading to road by start.

Optional riverside walk – 1 mile.

From fenced green, walk up Pound Hill and turn right at top along B4437. Descend pavement as far as lane on right, signposted Mill Field, Watery Lane and Pound Hill. At lane end, cross bridge and continue over meadow, passing W.D. Campbell memorial seat on left. At meadow end, cross footbridge on right and continue to reach kissing gate passed on main walk. Turn right and retrace steps to start.

Baptism in the Evenlode,

46

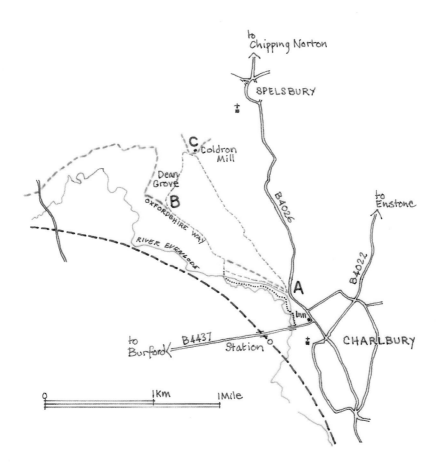

to
Chipping Norton

SPELSBURY

to
Enstone

B4026

B4022

C Coldron
Mill

Dean
Grove

B

OXFORDSHIRE WAY

RIVER EVENLODE

A

Inn

to
Burford

B4437

Station

CHARLBURY

0   1Km   1Mile

Public transport: Train to Charlbury.
Maps: O.S. Explorer 191 Banbury,
Bicester & Chipping Norton; O.S. Ex-
plorer OL 45 The Cotswolds.
Refreshments: Bell Hotel,Church St
(01608 810278), Bull Hotel,Market St
(01608 810689), Rose & Crown, Sheep
St (01608 810103); Ramble On café at
News and Things, Sheep St (01608
810228); all Charlbury

Walk 10: CHARLBURY, CORNBURY & FAWLER

Unlike the previous walk, this longer ramble passes through the centre of Charlbury, thus providing the opportunity to see something of the only town on the Evenlode.

The original settlement, known as Ceorl's burgh ('fortified town of free men') grew up on the

Beating the bounds, 1896: the eastern crossing

edge of the vast royal hunting forest of Wychwood, which was to exert a profound influence on the little town until its disafforestation in the mid 19th century. From 1094, the parish belonged to Eynsham Abbey and in 1109, the town received its charter from Henry I. St.Mary's church dates from that period, although its north arcade of three bays is all that survives of the original building.

Beyond the church, two other buildings of note are passed before the bridge over the Evenlode into Cornbury Park is reached. The first of these, on a bank to the left of the road, is the former grammar school, dating from 1837, and which served the town until 1911. Immediately beyond, and shielded by a wall and clipped yews, can be glimpsed Lee Place, a fine 17th century mansion named after the Lees of Ditchley, whose dower house it once was.

The walk skirts the edge of Cornbury Park, an extensive private estate that dates back to its establishment as the site of a royal hunting lodge in the 14th century. The oldest part of the present house is 16th century, although successive owners have enlarged and modified it considerably over the centuries. The house itself stands back from the footpath and is hidden from view by the trees, many of which are venerable old oaks. Later, a change of scene is provided by the easternmost extremity of a chain of artificial lakes, offering bird-watching opportunities.

The approach to the hamlet of Fawler cannot fail to delight the walker. An all-too-short stretch of riverside footpath reveals the Evenlode at its most beguiling before the route passes beneath the railway and enters the hamlet. Fawler owes its name to the Old English 'Fauflor', or coloured floor, relating to a mosaic forming part of a Roman villa,

Fawler

the remains of which were disturbed during the construction of the railway in 1852. Fawler was once the scene of considerable industrial activity, with ironstone quarries, limekilns, claypits and brick kilns, all of which ceased production many years ago.

Back at Charlbury, the final stage of the walk passes the Playing Close, a tree-fringed green mentioned in records dating back to the mid 15th century, when archery was practised here. Fairs were held on the Close for many years and the barbaric sport of bull-baiting went on until 1820. Alongside the Close stands a fountain presented to the town by John Kibble, a stonemason and local historian, to commemorate Queen Victoria's diamond jubilee.

A visit to the town's museum (open April to October Saturdays 10 - 12, Sundays and Bank Holiday Mondays 2.30 - 4.30) enables visitors to learn something of Charlbury's history, especially its former chief industry of glove-making.

Jubilee Memorial

Walk 10: CHARLBURY, CORNBURY & FAWLER
5 miles (2 ½ hours). Location: Charlbury. Start: Spendlove car park. (GR 358196).

A   From car park, walk down Browns Lane to crossroads. Go straight over down Church Street, passing church on right. Road descends to left, then climbs past former grammar school and grounds of Lee Place. Opposite lodge, turn right along drive (public footpath Finstock sign). Notice covered well on left. Route crosses railway and Evenlode before passing through door on left in front of lodge and cattle-grid.

B   Beyond door, cross stile to enter field. Route keeps Cornbury Park boundary fence on right. Continue to cross stile and follow track to pass lake on right. Route now follows private road, with wide grass verges, for about ¾ mile to reach Charlbury-Finstock road. At this point, turn left, then immediately right along concreted road. Beyond sewage works, route continues as grassy track for short distance, then as footpath over field. At field end, descend grassy bank to reach fork in path.

C   Take left hand fork. Pass through barrier and climb stile. Path crosses field between banks to reach stile by Evenlode. Delightful riverside path passes through woodland to footbridge. Cross river and continue beneath railway bridge and through handgates to follow lane into hamlet of Fawler. At road, turn left. Climb to reach track, concreted at first, on right, signposted 'Bridleway Charlbury'. Follow track for rather more than ½ mile to reach crossways of routes.

D   Turn left through gateway (blue waymark on post) along Oxfordshire Way. This mile-long stretch of the Way is a narrow hedged track affording glimpses of Finstock, Cornbury Park and Wychwood Forest through gaps at intervals. Way eventually emerges by houses and dips to left to reach B4437. Turn right (beware

The Oxfordshire Way

– no pavement). In 100 yards, turn left through kissing gate to follow public footpath, winding between gardens to reach estate road. Turn right, then left along estate road to reach main road.

E   Turn right. Pass fire station on right. Continue to reach Dancers Hill on left. Descend, then climb to pass green on right. Car park is opposite.

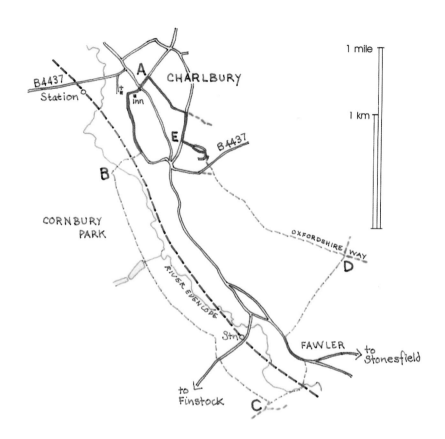

Roofed well in Cornbury Park

Public transport: Train to Charlbury.
Map: O.S. Explorer 180 Oxford Woodstock and Witney
Refreshments: Bell Hotel (01608 810278), Bull Hotel (01608 810689), Rose & Crown (01608 810103); all Charlbury

Walk 11: STONESFIELD & COMBE

Surprisingly, Stonesfield, widely famed for its Cotswold slates, owes its name, not to its geological associations but to one Stunta, a Saxon who made the place his home.

But for a scatter of 'Quarry (dis)' and 'Pit (dis)' marked on the map, there is little to remind us today of Stonesfield's once thriving industry, which was well established by the end of the 16th century and which extended until the early years of the 20th. Ironically, very few locally quarried slates can be seen on the village roofs, many having been sold and replaced by alien materials, while the waste from the pits and quarries was removed in the years following the second world war for road building.

Fortunately, the history of the industry has been well chronicled. In the early days the pendle, as the blocks of stone were called, was obtained from quarries but as these easily worked layers were exhausted, pits were sunk and the stone mined from a labyrinth of low galleries. On reaching the surface, the pendle was dampened, covered with straw and sealed under an earth clamp to await the first autumn frosts. On their arrival, the clamps were opened and the stone exposed to allow it to split into the wafer-like layers from which the slates were trimmed

A profitable sideline resulting from the quarrying was the sale of the rich variety of fossils embedded in the limestone. This trade prompted the Victorian travel writer Augustus Hare's scathing dismissal of Stonesfield: 'The wretched little village, in an exposed situation, consisting of a succession of fossil shops, containing specimens obtained in it.'

Leaving Stonesfield, the walk is a naturalist's paradise as it descends the sunken Brook Lane and crosses Stockey Bottom to reach and follow the Evenlode from Ashford Bridge. A succession of limestone-loving wild flowers gladden the way through spring and summer, while the Evenlode reveals its

North Leigh Roman villa

subtle charms as it loops northwards by Whitehill Wood before reverting to its south-easterly course to pass the Roman villa near East End.

This extensive site, the remains of a villa dating from the 2nd century AD, was excavated in 1815. Sadly, only one mosaic pavement has survived.

Combe, an attractive village grouped round a spacious green, is so called from the Celtic 'cumb', meaning 'at the valley', indicating that its original site was nearer the Evenlode, a fact confirmed by the writings of an 18th century antiquarian: 'Though the church and town be now upon a hill, yet was the church first built in the deep adjoining valley at the east end of the water mill.' (The

Hamo Thornycroft's Mower

successor to this mill features on Walk 14).

At the junction of Chatterpie Lane and West End stands The Old Farmhouse, which from May1923 until his death in December 1925 was the home of the sculptor Sir William (Hamo) Thornycroft, whose many celebrated works include the statue of Oliver Cromwell at Westminster and King Alfred at Winchester. A commemorative stone in the house wall can be seen from the road, above a niche in which once stood a small statuette by Thornycroft of 'A mower whetting his scythe'.

Notable among the many distinguished visitors to Combe at this time was the sculptor's nephew, the poet Siegfried Sassoon. Describing one such visit made in July 1923, Sassoon recalled: 'He took me down to the Evenlode, where he had a canoe. . . We navigated the reed-choked and willow-cumbered little river with high gusto, Uncle H getting out and wading a lot. He would have played any boyish game on that river, pretending that we were explorers'.

The present church of St Laurence was built by Eynsham Abbey sometime in the 14th century and contains a fine medieval stone pulpit and a series of 15th century wall paintings, together with stained glass from the same period.

Beyond Combe, the walk enters the western extremity of Blenheim Park before joining the Oxfordshire Way, routed along the course of the Roman Akeman Street, leading back over fields to Stonesfield.

Walk 11: STONESFIELD & COMBE

7 miles (3½ hours). Location: Stonesfield. The village lies 3 miles west of Woodstock. Start: Small parking area near church (GR 395171).

A   Leaving parking area (with church, lockup and post office close by), follow road to right. (Black Head inn can be seen away to left). When road swings to right, continue straight on along Brook Lane, with cemetery on right. Pass concrete posts and descend steps. At foot of slope, instead of crossing footbridge, turn right. Keep left at fork and climb to handgate. Keep to right along open ground with bushes and trees on right. Continue to reach road via gate.

Akeman Street approaches the Evenlode

B   Turn left. Cross railway bridge and continue to cross Evenlode at Ashford Bridge. At crossroads, turn left (East End and Hanborough signpost). In 30 yards, take footpath on left (Stonesfield signpost). This follows Evenlode, with woodland on right at first, then passes under railway bridge. Beyond stile, turn right along grassy track. Go through gate and over railway bridge to reach track on left leading to Roman villa.

C   Cross stile to left of villa entrance. Keep hedge on right. Cross plank bridge and stile to reach Evenlode near railway bridge. Go under bridge and continue along river bank to reach and cross gated cart bridge. Follow climbing track to pass through farm. Continue along lane, passing sewage works. Lane soon climbs to reach Combe. Keep right in village, then left at fork (School sign on right). Pass village green and Cock Inn on left and cedar tree and church on right. Continue to reach public footpath, signposted Combe Steps, on left, 30 yards beyond derestriction sign.

D   Cross field to reach hedge and keep it on left as far as Blenheim Park wall. Turn left along wall as far as step-stile into Park. Follow clear track to left for about a mile, passing Mapleton Pond on right, to reach Oxfordshire Way.

E   Turn left to leave Park over step-stile. Follow Oxfordshire Way over fields. Cross road and continue as far as another. Leave Oxfordshire Way here. Turn right along this road and climb back to Stonesfield. On reaching war memorial, turn left and left again back to start.

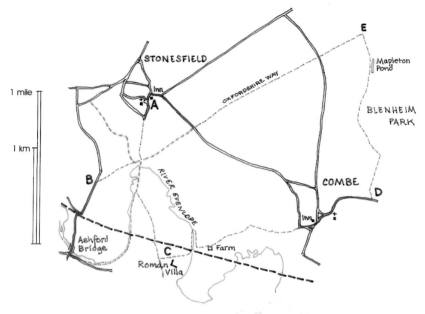

STONESFIELD

Inn

A

OXFORDSHIRE WAY

E

Mapleton Pond

BLENHEIM PARK

COMBE

D

Inn

1 mile

1 km

B

RIVER EVENLODE

Ashford Bridge

C

Roman Villa

Farm

Stonesfield lock--up

Map: O.S. Explorer 180 Oxford Witney and Woodstock.
Refreshments: Black Head, Stonesfield (01993 891616); Cock Inn, Combe (01993 891288).

Walk 12: THE GLYME VALLEY

As its title indicates, the route of this walk explores the valley of the Evenlode's most substantial tributary, the Glyme, on the last stage of its journey before entering Blenheim Park. This delightful little river, flowing south-eastwards from its source above Chipping Norton, graces the villages of Enstone, Kiddington and Glympton before wrig-

Wootton Bridge

gling its way beneath loftily perched Wootton. Here it receives the waters of an even more modest river, the Dorn, flowing due south from the Barton villages on a course roughly parallel to that of a river of far greater consequence, the Cherwell, away to the east.

Modest it may be, but the Glyme's charms were once praised in verse by no less a figure than a poet laureate. Thomas Warton, rector of tiny Kiddington from 1771 until his death in 1790, was an Oxford scholar whose reputation as a poet was established early in life. In 1785, the same year that he received the laureateship, his qualities as an historian led to his being appointed Camden Professor of History.

Warton's scholarship in history was not confined to the

Kilvert plaque in Wootton church

national stage. In 1783, he published *A History of Kiddington*, which proved so popular that it was reprinted many years after his death. In it, he describes the Glyme as 'a deep but narrow stream, winding through willowed meadows and abounding in trout and wild fowl.'

The young Glyme winds through the meadows

It is in Warton's April Ode, composed in his beloved Kiddington, that the river which beautifies the village appears;

> Within some whispering osier isle,
> Where Glyme's low banks neglected smile,
> And each trim meadow still retains
> The wintry torrent's oozy stains.
> O'er the broad downs, a novel race,
> Frisk the young lambs with faltering pace,
> And with eager bleating fill
> The Foss that skirts the beaconed hill.

The approach to Wootton crosses Stratford Lane (Via Strata – paved way) a section of Roman Akeman Street that linked Cirencester with St. Albans. The Glyme can be glimpsed nearby as it flows beneath Stratford Bridge, first referred to in 1279.

The suggested extension into Wootton is well worth the effort. Deriving its name from 'settlement in a wood', the village was once within Wychwood Forest and its stone-built houses, steep streets and handsome church give it a rare distinctiveness. It was in this church, as a wall plaque reminds us, that the Rev. Francis Kilvert was married to Elizabeth Anne Rowland, of Wootton. The celebrated diarist, vicar of Bredwardine, Herefordshire, was to live a mere five weeks longer, dying of peritonitis on 23rd September, 1879, aged 38.

Hordley, formerly a hamlet of Wootton, is now merely a farm, but the house itself, built around the three and a half sides of a courtyard, dates from around 1500, although it was remodelled in the mid 18th century.

Sansom's Farm, standing at the intersection of Akeman Street and the B4027, was the site of a toll house in the 18th century when the latter was a turnpiked section of the road linking London and Aberystwyth. It now houses the Oxford Stage School.

Walk 12: THE GLYME VALLEY

5 miles (4¼ miles omitting Wootton) 2½ or 3½ hours. Location: Woodstock. Start: Town centre. (GR 445167). Street parking or car park off Hensington Road..

A   Walk north along A44 (right hand pavement). Cross bridge over River Glyme .Pass Black Prince inn and climb as far as barrier by phone box. Turn right along Westland Way and immediately left along Rosamund Drive. At end of drive, follow footpath signposted Wootton. Path skirts playground and swings to right along fence before striking off across large field. In next field, pass barns on left. Wootton church visible ahead. At field end, cross stile into thicket and descend to road. (Stratford Lane). Picturesque views from Stratford Bridge short distance downhill to right.

B   Cross stile opposite and continue up bank towards wood. Keep this on left to cross stile. Beyond hedge gap, keep hedge on right. Cross track and continue through handgate and down bank to reach cross path, with finger post indicating left.

C   To visit Wootton, follow direction indicated by finger post, down sunken lane to road. Turn right at foot, cross bridge over Glyme and climb to village. Retrace steps to finger post.

To continue route, turn right at finger post (no waymark) and cross top of sloping field, passing house on right. Pass through Long Meadow nature reserve (confluence of rivers Dorn and Glyme

near far extremity of nature reserve, to left of private footbridge). Keep straight on to cross footbridge and reach drive, with Hordley farmhouse on right. Short way up drive, go through gate on right. Second gate leads into field. Cross, aiming for buildings (Sansoms Farm).

D   On reaching B4027, follow it to right (no pavement). In 100 yards, turn right into field (no waymark). Keep hedge on right to join track. Turn right along it. Keep right at fork and follow hedged track (later surfaced road) back into Woodstock.

Snowdrops near Hordley

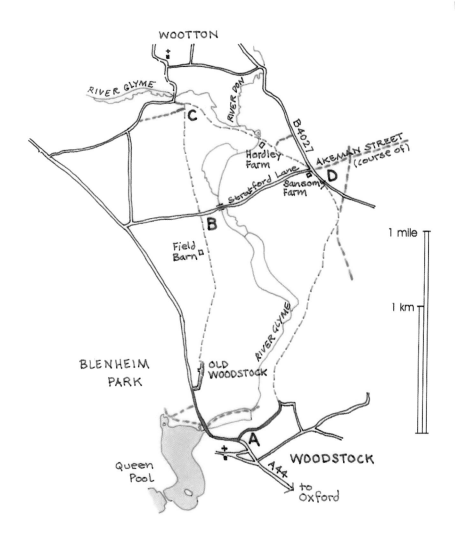

Public transport: Train to Oxford; then bus to Woodstock.
Map: O.S. Explorer 180 Oxford Witney and Woodstock.
Refreshments: King's Head, Wootton (01993 811340); numerous inns and teashops in Woodstock.

Walk 13: BLENHEIM PARK

Blenheim Park: the lake

Although the Evenlode merely skirts the south-western boundary of Blenheim Park before receiving the waters of its principal tributary, the Glyme, no study of the river can ignore the presence nearby of a 2000-acre park containing a magnificent palace built to honour a national hero.

The story of the building of Blenheim Palace is too well known to need repeating here. Sufficient to say that although the architect Sir John Vanbrugh was responsible for building the Grand Bridge spanning the little river Glyme in 1712, it was over 50 years later that the fourth Duke of Marlborough brought in the celebrated Lancelot 'Capability' Brown to create the park as we know it today. In the words of one writer:

'At Blenheim, Capability Brown really let himself go, damming up the Glyme to ally nature and artifice in the forming of the lake, and magnificently playing about with the landscape in a god-like way.'

Much of Blenheim Park is open to all walkers, with rights of way well marked on ordnance survey maps. The Glyme falls within that part of the grounds for which an admission charge is made, but the views which one has from its banks make it well worth the expense, especially at those times when the crowds are thinner. One has the added benefit of being able to walk across the water terraces beside the palace on one's way to the edge of the lake.

At the eastern end of the lake the Glyme emerges over a waterfall (the 'Grand Cascade') before passing on towards Bladon Bridge and sweeping in a great arc to meet the Evenlode. The walk turns back towards the palace, passing some picturesque features of the grounds, such as the Arboretum, the Rose garden and the Temple of Diana, with its plaque commemorating the betrothal of Winston and Clementine Churchill.

Bladon bridge, though not traversed by this walk, can be accessed from the drive leading from the palace towards Bladon, which continues as an outer route through the park, skirting the lake on its farther side. Though lacking the prominent splendour of Grand Bridge, it is nevertheless an elegant structure, consisting of three noble arches with a balustraded parapet. It was built in 1773, its architect being William Chambers. Brown is also credited with the rebuilt, Gothic-style High Lodge, with its embattled central tower, passed on the outer route, built as the residence of the ranger of the park..

Other walks in the park reveal that sufficient natural woodland – the eastern extremity of the ancient forest of Wychwood - has survived around Combe Lodge and in High Park to provide a pleasing contrast with Brown's contrived landscaping. This remnant of old Wychwood takes the form of an impressive array of oaks, many still in fine condition, others reduced through the ravages of time to leafless, hollow giants, their huge lifeless boughs providing ideal nesting sites for owls and jackdaws.

The Grand Cascade

Walk 13: BLENHEIM PARK

2½ miles (1¼ hours). Location: Woodstock. Start: Town centre (GR 445167). Street parking or free car park off Hensington Road.

A   Start at the Woodstock gate to the park (The 'Triumphal Arch'), where you will need to buy your ticket, but do not proceed through the gate. Instead, turn back and take the first turning on the left, called Chaucer's Lane (the house on the corner is 'Chaucer's House', the home of Thomas Chaucer, Speaker of the House of Commons in the fifteenth century and (possibly) the son of Geoffrey. Where the road bends right, continue straight on down the steps. At the bottom turn left and walk north along A44 (left hand pavement). Cross bridge over River Glyme and go through high door on left. A second door leads into Blenheim Park. Turn left along drive and cross the river; then follow left bank, with the palace and Vanbrugh's bridge ahead of you. The water on your right is known as the Queen's Pool. At the picnic site, bear left up the slope towards palace and enter courtyard through main entrance. Proceed straight on into main courtyard in front of the palace, and go diagonally across this towards the door marked as the entrance to the gardens. This leads to the Water Terraces.

Column of Victory

B Exit from upper terrace by the steps on the left-hand side. Half-way along left-hand side of the lower terrace go up four steps on left, followed by a wide gravel path. At the end of this turn right and in about 50 yards right again at a sign marked 'Lakeside Walk'. In a short distance another sign directs you sharply to the left and down slope towards the lake. The walk now follows the lake, past half-timbered boathouse and below some fine cedars to where the lake narrows and a footbridge marked 'Private' crosses it. Path continues round the left-hand bend, with the sound of

the cascade ever louder. Pass small building on the right (the Pump House) to get the full view of the Grand Cascade from the foot bridge.

C Path continues along the river for a short distance but then diverges from it, as the latter continues on towards Bladon Bridge. Path rises up a slope with a ha-ha on the right and fine specimen tress on the left. It passes the Rose Garden on the left and the Temple of Diana. Eventually it leads back to the Water Terraces.

D Retrace your steps across the terraces and the courtyards to main entrance; then follow the drive, bearing left at the crossroads towards the Woodstock gate and your starting point.

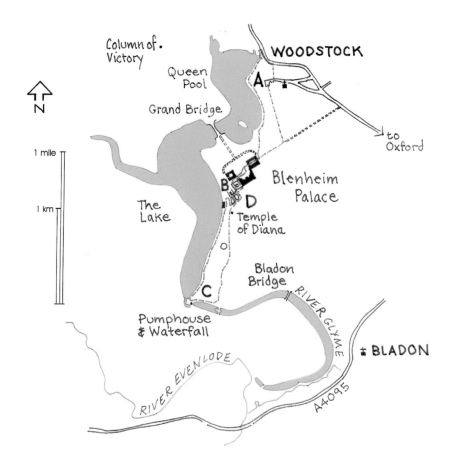

To extend the walk turn right at the crossroads and walk towards the entrance to the Pleasure Gardens leaving this on your right. Follow the drive to a lodge on your right, and there turn right to go down to Bladon Bridge. It is possible to walk a complete circuit of the park (about four miles) by continuing along the drives through High Park, past High Lodge and Combe Lodge and down to an inlet of the lake, before rising again to pass by the Column of Victory and back to the gate where you entered the park.

Public transport: Train to Oxford; then bus to Woodstock.
Map O.S. Explorer 180 Oxford Witney and Woodstock
Refreshments: Blenheim Palace; Oxfordshire Museum, Woodstock (01993 811456) ; numerous Inns and teashops in Woodstock. .

Walk 14: LONG HANBOROUGH CIRCULAR

The two Hanboroughs - Long and Church – are so named from the Old English 'Hane's or Hanna's Hill.' Although it is the prettier and more compact Church Hanborough that finds favour in the guidebooks, Long Hanborough has a closer affinity with the River Evenlode, being well served by footpaths and bridleways leaving the bustling main street for the quiet fields.

to Osney Abbey. Known locally as Folly Bridge, it featured in a dramatic incident at dawn on 4th June 1644, when King Charles I,

The old bridge, Long Hanborough

This main street, now the A4095 Witney –Woodstock road, is not without interest. There are a number of well-built Cotswold stone houses and inns, together with the former manor house, standing back from the road. Before the turnpiking of this road, in 1751, the section near the manor was closed to traffic once a year for the Hanborough Feast. At that time, the bridge spanning the Evenlode at the eastern edge of the village was an ancient structure dating originally from 1141, when Empress Maud granted land by the river (then known as the Bladen) at Long Hanborough

having led his army secretly on a night march from Oxford, crossed the Evenlode and drew up on Hanborough Heath before making for Burford. This bridge, rebuilt in 1798, still stands, midway between the two unclassified roads heading south from the A 4095. It was finally replaced in 1954 when the siting of its successor removed an awkward bend in the road at the approach to Bladon.

The fields to the north of Long Hanborough, through which the route passes, were enclosed in 1773. Apart from the coming of the railway 80 years later, they have changed little since that time, ensuring that the Evenlode, snaking towards its meeting with the Glyme on the edge of Blenheim Park, retains its former charm. Little trace remains of the quarries that scarred the southern slopes of the valley since medieval times, although the last of these, which yielded stone for the building of the Oxford University Press building in the 1820s and for Eynsham Hall, remained open until 1904.

Another once thriving local industry was brick-making. This took place around Hanborough Heath, in the west of the parish and there is a record of a Hanborough brickworks producing half a million bricks for the building of the walls around the newly-established kitchen gardens at Blenheim Palace in 1706. As with quarrying, the industry continued until the early years of the 20th century.

Approaching Combe station on the latter stages of the walk, a glimpse can be had of the chimney and associated buildings of Combe mill. This historic site, already referred to in the text relating to Walk 11, was where the village of Combe once stood, a Saxon corn mill having been recorded here in Domesday Book. The present mill, built at about the time of the coming of the railway in 1853, served as a sawmill for the Blenheim estate and contains a splendid beam engine in full working order, driven by what is believed to be the oldest working boiler in the country. Between 1912 and 1972, the mill engine remained idle, although the water

Beam engine, Combe

wheel functioned until the 1950s, when electric power was installed. However, thanks to the endeavours of a group of enthusiastic volunteers, the beam engine and boiler were finally restored and the mill opened to visitors at weekends in 1975.

Walk 14: LONG HANBOROUGH CIRCULAR

4¼ miles (2 hours).Location: Long Hanborough. Village stands on B4095 between Witney and Woodstock. Start: Park Lane.(left side of A4095, between George & Dragon inn and railway station) GR 428 143.

A Walk down Park Lane (No through road and no turning for cars). Lane eventually becomes bridleway and enters field. Keep hedge on right as far as gap. Pass through this and continue with hedge on left. At field end, go through handgate on left and follow track to road. Turn left (no pavement) and continue as far as handgate on right alongside entrance to industrial establishment.

B Follow footpath into wood. Ignore bridge on right. Keep on along woodland path, ignoring another footbridge, also on right. On reaching fence straight ahead, turn right to leave wood and in 10 yards, veer to left to follow path skirting woodland. Railway bridge comes into view in distance ahead. Climb slope, following woodland edge At top of slope, path becomes track and enters wood. Ignore handgate on right and continue past garden fences on left to reach cross-track.

C Turn right and follow woodland edge. At wood corner, follow grassy track round to right, with newly-planted woodland on left. Ignore path leading towards cottages away to left and continue to right along woodland edge to cross footbridge. Route continues over field, with

Evenlode on right, to cross river at Grintley Hill Bridge. Beyond, climb track to left to cross bridge over railway and continue to join road.

D Turn right along road. Pass railway station

Swan family near Long Hanborough

approach to reach T-junction. Turn right. Pass lane to sawmill on right and continue to cross Evenlode and reach bridleway on left, walked on outward route. Retrace steps to start.

Public transport: Train to Hanborough.
Map O.S. Explorer 180 Oxford Witney and Woodstock
Refreshments: Bell Inn, Hanborough (01993 881324).

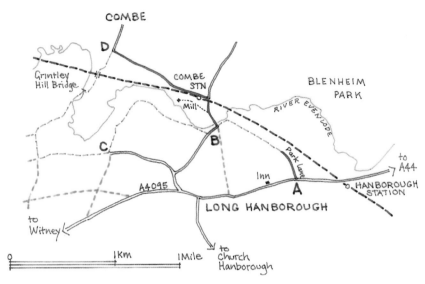

COMBE

D

Grintley Hill Bridge

COMBE STN

Mill

BLENHEIM PARK

RIVER EVENLODE

C

B

Park Lane

to A44

Inn

A

to HANBOROUGH STATION

A4095

LONG HANBOROUGH

to Witney

0   1Km   1Mile

to Church Hanborough

Combe Bridge

Walk 15: CASSINGTON AND THE THAMES

Looking towards Church Hanborough

Evenlode from its earliest beginnings near Moreton-in-Marsh, finally deserts the valley a short distance beyond Hanborough station, sweeping away south-eastwards on its way to Oxford.

Although present-day settlements between Long Hanborough and Cassington are confined to a handful of isolated farms, there is archeological evidence that this stretch of the Evenlode valley was inhabited in prehistoric times. Excavations near Purwell Farm, passed on the accompanying walk, have revealed Bronze Age burials and early Iron Age occupation,

Always something of an elusive river, the Evenlode seems to shun human contact beyond its confluence with its tributary the Glyme, for the rest of its journey to the Thames below Cassington. Not only are riverside footpaths totally absent, apart from a short stretch downstream of Eynsham Mill, but access points of any kind between the latter and the Thames are confined to two – that near Goose Eye Farm (see walk directions) and from the last bridge over the river on Cassington Road. Even the railway, close companion of the

Wharf Farm and canal

as well as evidence of a Saxon village.

Cassington, the last village in the vicinity of the Evenlode, is a pleasant enough place, with ancient spire-topped church, green neatly bisected by a row of fine limes and an attractive blend of old and new buildings.

The Evenlode flows into the Thames

However, it is separated from the river by the A40, along which traffic thunders without respite, leaving the Evenlode to meander its final mile through a sprawl of industrial ugliness from which the public is mercifully excluded.

Cassington Mill, the last on the Evenlode, and now engulfed by this wasteland, was for some time the administrative centre of a caravan park. Until 1938, it had been a flour mill and stands on the site of a mill recorded in Domesday Book, which is said to have paid a tax of 175 eels per year.

From Cassington Road, not far from the last bridge spanning the Evenlode, is another bridge alongside Wharf Farm. As its name indicates, the farm was built to serve a half-mile canal, dug by a former Duke of Marlborough to enable locally produced malt and corn to be transported along the Thames to Oxford and coal and timber brought inland to Cassington, Eynsham and neighbouring villages.

Like the Evenlode itself, the point at which the canal joins the Thames can be seen from a particularly scenic stretch of the Thames Path. This can be reached at Swinford Lock, just downstream from the bridge of the same name, which still exacts a toll from each passing vehicle, much as the ferry did which it replaced in 1769. An interesting route to the Thames Path can be taken from the Talbot Inn, at the site of Eynsham wharf, going down the wharf stream which now runs alongside the huge workshop of Oxford Magnetic Technology Ltd. and over the weir and lock; then to walk downstream between the river and the northern extremity of Wytham Wood. This, the backdrop to the last section of the Evenlode, extends almost to the river bank.

Walk 15a: CASSINGTON

3 miles (1¼ hours) involving retracing steps. Location: Cassington. Village lies off A40, 2 miles NE of Eynsham. Start: Village street, opposite approach to church and by 30 sign. (GR 453107). Street parking.

A   Follow public footpath sign along gravel drive. Footpath continues to left of house as wide track with hedge on right. Beyond watercourse, path keeps hedge on left at first, then continues straight on along bank. When track veers to left towards Purwell Farm, keep straight on to pass through 2 gates and reach surfaced lane. Turn left for short distance then follow hedge round to right, passing farmhouse away to left. On reaching hedge descending to left, follow it down to bottom corner. Go through gap and cross field to river bank.

B   Retrace steps back to start.

Walk 15b: THE THAMES

3¼ miles (1½ hours) involving retracing steps. Location: Swinford Bridge, Eynsham (GR 440088). Street parking in Wharf Road, just N of Talbot Inn.

C   Start from Talbot Inn carpark: take signed footpath through carpark and along bank of Wharf Stream next to long factory building. At end of building continue to follow stream and go through metal kissing gate into field. Remain beside stream through this field and into next. Look out for footbridge over stream on right and climb two stiles to reach this. Cross bridge into field and head diagonally across field towards lock. At river, cross weir by footbridge and lock by gates. Turn left on to Thames Path and follow path for about a mile to see the confluence, marked with a signboard.

D   Retrace steps back to start.

Cassington green

70

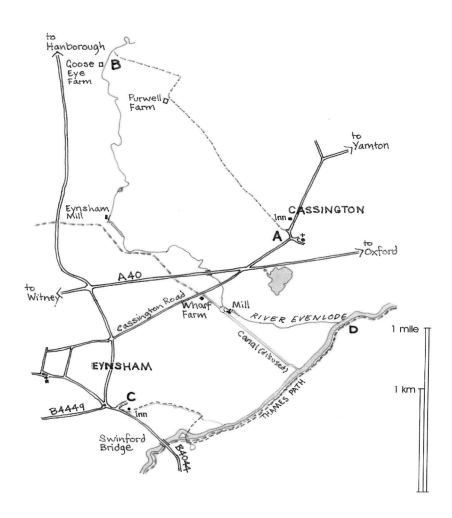

Map O.S. Explorer 180 Oxford Witney
and Woodstock
Refreshments: Red Lion, Chequers
Cassington; Talbot, Eynsham.

The Evenlode and the railway

When the Oxford, Worcester and Wolverhampton railway was laid out in 1845 the natural choice of route between Oxford and Worcester was up the gently sloping valley of the Evenlode to Moreton in Marsh, and then sharply down the Cotswold escarpment through Campden Tunnel into the Vale of Evesham. Thus the Evenlode intertwines with the railway for most of its course and, apart from giving the rail traveller some of the best glimpses of this otherwise rather private river, this allows access to most of the walks in this book by rail, or by one of the growing number of rail-bus connections.

The means of reaching the start and finish points of each walk by public transport are shown on the itinerary pages. For the traveller who desires a compressed view of the Evenlode a trip by rail from Oxford to Moreton in Marsh shows practically the whole river in a little over half an hour. In summer there are enchanting views of the sleepy stream, overhung with foliage, winding from side to side of the railway, which crosses it eleven times betwen Hanborough and Charlbury; but the views in winter are no less impressive, and rather more extensive through the leafless vegetation.

Sitting on the left-hand side of the train, going away from Oxford, the first sight of the river comes just before Hanborough station, just below its confluence with the Glyme as the latter emerges from Blenheim Park. Beyond Hanborough the Evenlode describes a series of graceful arcs on either side of the track, all the way to Charlbury. Between there and Kingham the railway runs parallel and close to several of the walks in this book. About three minutes beyond Kingham the railway passes under a road bridge and past the now unmarked site of Adlestrop station (see page 20). Above here the railway and river continue their flirtation, but sharper eyes are needed now to spot the Evenlode, at this point only a few feet across. The last sighting is as the houses of Moreton come into view, although you can look up at the ridge to the west to see the spring line where the Evenlode starts to gather its waters.

WORKS CONSULTED

J.L.R. Anderson	*The Upper Thames.* Eyre & Spottiswoode 1970
M.K. Ashby	*The Changing English Village 1066-1914.* Roundwood 1974
Robert & Monica Beckinsale	*The English Heartland.* Duckworth 1980.
John Betjeman	*Summoned by Bells.* John Murray 1960
Christine Bloxham	*Portrait of Oxfordshire* Hale 1982
Joanna Cannan	*Oxfordshire.* Hale1975
Herbert Evans	*Highways & Byways in Oxford & The Cotswolds.* Macmillan1908.
David Green	*Country Neighbours.* Blandford 1948.
Frederick Grisewood	*The World Goes By.* Secker & Warburg 1952
Nigel Hammond	*The Oxfordshire Village Book.* Countryside Books 1983
Anne Harvey	*Adlestrop Revisited.* Sutton 1999
Lois Hey	*A History of Charlbury.* Wychwood Press 2001
Robert Hill	*A Short History of Charlbury.* Privately published 1975
Mary & Ken Jackson	*W.D.Campbell - Naturalist & Teacher.* Wychwood Press 2003
Charles Keighley	*Discovering Wychwood.* Wychwood Press 2000
S.P.B. Mais	*Our Village Today.* Werner Laurie 1956
R.M.Marshall	*Oxfordshire Byways.* Alden Press 1935
H.J. Massingham	*Wold Without End.* Cobden Sanderson 1932
	Cotswold Country. Batsford 1937
	Shepherd's Country. Chapman & Hall 1938
Arthur Mee	*Gloucestershire.* Hodder & Stoughton 1938
	Oxfordshire. Hodder & Stoughton 1942
Gordon Ottewell	*Warde Fowler's Countryside.* Severn House 1985
	Gloucestershire Countryside. Minton & Minton 1991
	Discovering Cotswold Villages Sigma Press 1997
Roy Palmer	*The Folklore of Gloucestershire.* Westcountry Books 1994
Nikolaus Pevsner & Jennifer Sherwood	*Oxfordshire.* Penguin 1974
A.H.Smith	*The Place Names of Gloucestershire. (Parts 1 & 4)* CUP 1964
Mary Sturge Gretton	*Three Centuries in North Oxfordshire.* Edward Arnold 1902
	A Corner of the Cotswolds. Methuen 1914
Edward Thomas	*Horae Solitariae.* Duckworth 1902
Reginald Turnor	*Oxfordshire.* Paul Elek 1949
Charles Tyzack	*Wychwood & Cornbury.* Wychwood Press 2003
David Verey	*Gloucestershire: The Cotswolds.* Penguin 1970
Victoria County History	*Gloucestershire.* OUP 1968
	Oxfordshire. OUP 1968
William Warde Fowler	*A Year With the Birds.* Blackwell 1887
	Kingham Old & New. Blackwell 1913
Brian Waters	*Thirteen Rivers to the Thames.* Dent 1964
Mary Webb et al	*Evenlode & Wychwood.* Oxfordshire Books 1990
	Glyme Valley. Artisan Press 1997
Ethel Carleton Williams	*Companion into Oxfordshire.* Methuen 1935
Marilyn Yurdan	*Oxfordshire & Oxford.* Shire Publications 1988
	Discovering Literary Oxfordshire The Book Castle 2003

Index

A

"A History of Kiddington" 57
Aberystwyth 57
Adlestrop 20, 22
Adlestrop Park 20
"Adlestrop Revisited" 20
Akeman Street 53, 57
April Ode 57
Armada Cottage, Charlbury 45
Ascott Castle 36, 40
Ascott D'Oyley 36, 40
Ascott Earl 36, 38
"Ascott Martyrs" 37
Ascott under Wychwood 36, 40
Ashford Bridge, Stonesfield 52, 54
Austen, Jane 20

B

Batsford Park 16
Beauchamp family 32
Belloc, Hilaire 8
Benfield, Charles 29
Berks, Bucks and Oxon Wildlife Trust 29
Betjeman, John 12
Bladintyn 28
Bladon 7
Bladon Bridge, Blenheim 61
Bledington 6, 25, 28
Bledington Heath 24
Bledington Hey Away, dance 29
Bledington Mill 29
Blenheim estate 65
Blenheim Palace 60, 65
Blenheim Park 53, 54, 60, 62, 65
"Book of Martyrs" 32

Bosbury 22
Bould 29, 30
Bould Wood 29, 30
Bourton House 13, 14
Bourton-on-the-Hill 13, 14
Bourton-on-the-Water 29
Bridges
    Ashford, Stonesfield 52, 54
    Catsham 41
    Combe 67
    Folly, Hanborough 64
    Grand, Blenheim 60
    Grintley Hill 66
    Standbow 33
    Stratford, Evenlode 18
    Stratford, Wootton 58
Broadwell 16
Brook Lane, Stonesfield 52, 54
Brown, Lancelot 'Capability 60
Browns Lane, Charlbury 50
Bruern Abbey 32, 33, 34
Brunel, Isambard Kingdom 7
Burford 64

C

Campbell, W.D. 45, 46
Cassington 68
Cassington Mill 69
Cassington Road 68
Catsham Bridge 41
Catsham Lane 42
Ceorl 48
Chambers, William 61
Charlbury 7, 44, 48, 50
Charlbury Grammar School 48
Charlbury Museum 49
Charles I 64
Chastleton 17
Chastleton House 17
Cherwell, River 56
Chilson 41, 42

Chipping Campden 8
Chipping Norton 25, 56
  Tweed Mill 25
Christ Church College, Oxford 33
Church Hanborough *64*
Church Street, Charlbury 50
Churches
  Adlestrop *20*
  Ascott under Wychwood 36
  Bledington 28, 29
  Bourton-on-the-Hill 13
  Charlbury 40
  Combe 53
  Daylesford 22
  Evenlode 17
  Longborough 12, 14
  Oddington 21
  Shipton under Wychwood 32, 34
  Shorthampton 41, 42
Churn, River 6
Cistercians 33
Cockerell, S P 12
Cockerell, Sir Charles 12
Cocksmoor Wood 33
Coldicote Farm 17
Coldron Brook 45
Coldron Mill 45, 46
Coldwell Brook 37
Coln, River 6
Combe 53, 54
Combe Mill *65*
Combe station *65*
Combe Steps 54
Cornbury Park 48, 50
Cospatrick, SS 32
"Cotswold Country" 8
Coxmoor, meadow 25, 26
Cozens Lane 26

D

Dancers Hill, Charlbury 50

Daniell, Thomas 13
Daniell, William 13
D'Arcy Dalton Way 34
Daylesford 20, 21, 22, 24, 26
Daylesford House 21
Dean Grove 45, 46
Diamond Way 18
Ditchley 48
Domesday Book 12, 28, *65*, *69*
Dorn, River 56, *58*
Drayton, Michael 7
Duckery 14
Dugdale, F B 12
Dugdale family 12
Dugdale, John 12

E

East End 53, 54
East India Company 12, 21
Enstone 56
Evans, Herbert 28
Evenlode village 16, 18
Eynsham *69*
Eynsham Abbey 40, 48
Eynsham Hall *65*
Eynsham Mill *68*

F

Fauflor 48
Fawler 48, 50
Finstock 50
Folly Bridge, Hanborough *64*
Foscot 29
Fosse Way 12
Fowler, William Warde 8, 24
Foxe, John 32
Foxholes 30, 32
Foxholes Farm 29
Foxholes Nature Reserve 29, 33

G

Gibbs, Edwin 29
Glyme, River 7, 56, *58*, *62*, *68*
Glympton 56
Goose Eye Farm *68*
Grand Bridge, Blenheim *60*
Great Western Railway 7
Grintley Hill Bridge *66*
Grisewood, Freddy 21

H

Hailes Abbey 12
Hanborough 54, *64*, *68*
Hanborough Feast *64*
Hanborough Heath *64*
Hane's Hill *64*
Hanna's Hill *64*
Hare, Augustus 52
Harvey, Anne 20
Hastings, Warren 21
Heart of England Way 12, 14
Henley-on-Thames *29*
Henry I 48
Heritage Lane, Ascott 38
High Park, Blenheim *61*
High Street, Ascott 41
"Highways and Byways Oxford and the
    Cotswolds" *28*
"Horae Solitariae" 8
Hordley *57*, *58*

I

Icomb 24
Inns
    Black Head, Stonesfield 54
    Coach and Horses, Bourton-on-the-Hill
        14
    Coach and Horses, Longborough 15
    Cock Inn, Combe 54
    Fox, Moreton-in-Marsh 19
    Fox, Oddington 22
    Horse and Groom, Bourton-on-the-Hill
        13
    King's Arms, Bledington 30
    Shaven Crown, Shipton 32
    Talbot, Eynsham 69, 70

J

Jackdaws *61*
Jenkinson family 44
Jenkinson, Robert, Earl of Liverpool 44

K

Ketford 46
Kibble, John 49
Kiddington 56
Kingfishers 33
Kingham 7, 16, 24, 26
Kingham Hill 24
"Kingham Old and New" 8, *24*
Kingham station 24

L

Lacy family 37
Langley Mill 36
Leach, River 6
Leadington 34
Ledbury 30
Lee family 48
Lee Place 48, 50
Leigh, James Henry *20*
Leigh, Sir William 12
Lincoln College, Oxford 8
Lockwood, Rev. 16
Long Hanborough *64*, *68*
Long Meadow Nature Reserve *58*
Longborough 12, 14
Lower Oddington Ashes, wood 26
Lyneham 32

M

Manor Farm, Ascott 42
Manor Farm, Bledington 29
Manor farmhouse, Bourton-on-the-Hill 13
"Mansfield Park" *20*
Mapleton Pond 54
Marlborough, Duke of *60, 69*
Massingham, HJ 8
Maud, Empress *64*
Meadow Lane, Shipton 34
Mill Field, Charlbury 46
Mill Lane, Ascott 41
Mill Lane, Chilson 41
Mills
    Bledington 29
    Bliss, Chipping Norton 25
    Cassington *69*
    Coldron 45, 46
    Combe 65
    Eynsham *68*
    Langley 36
Monarch's Way 14
Moreton-in-Marsh 7, 14, 16, 18, *68*
Morgan family 33
Morris dancing 29

N

New Zealand 32

O

Oddington 20, 22
Old Talbot, Charlbury 45
"On the Evenlode" 8
Osney Abbey *64*
Owls *61*
Oxford *64, 68*
Oxford Stage School 57
Oxford University Press 65
Oxford, Worcester & Wolverhampton
    Railway 7

Oxfordshire Way
    29, 30, 33, 34, 36, 38, 40, 44, 50, 53, 54

P

Palmer, Richard 13
Park Lane, Hanborough *66*
Pevsner, Nikolaus 41
Playing Close, Charlbury 49
Poly-Olbion 7
Poplars Farm, Evenlode 18
Pound Hill, Charlbury 45, 46
Prebendal House 33
Priory Farm 34
Pudlicote 40
Pudlicote House 40
Pudlicote Lane, Ascott 42
Purwell Farm, Cassington *68, 70*

R

Ramblers' Association 18
Redesdale, Lord 16
Roman villas
    Fawler 48
    North Leigh 53, 54
Rosamund Drive, Woodstock *58*

S

Sansom's Farm *57, 58*
Sars Brook *34*
Sassoon, Siegfried 53
School Lane, Chilson 42
Sezincote 12
Sezincote House 14
Sezincote Park 12
Sharp, Cecil 29
Shipton Court 37
Shipton-under-Wychwood 32, 36
Shorthampton 41, 42
St. Frideswide 41
St. George 41

St. Leonard 41
St. Zita 41
Standbow Bridge 33
Stock Bridge, Evenlode 16
Stockey Bottom, Stonesfield 52
Stonesfield 52, 54
Stonesfield slates 52
Stow-on-the-Wold 14, 24
Stratford Bridge, Evenlode 17, 18
Stratford Bridge, Wootton *58*
Stratford Lane, Woodstock *58*
Stunta 52
Swailsford Brook 25
Swinford Lock 69

T

Taston Brook 45
Thames Path 69, 70
Thames, River 7, *68*
"The World Goes By" *21*
Thomas, Edward 8, 20
Thornton Lacey *20*
Thornycroft, Sir William 53
Tristan da Cunha 32

V

Vanbrugh, Sir John *60*

W

Walcot 44
Warton, Thomas 56
Water voles 33
Watery Lane, Charlbury 46
Westcote Brook 29, 30
Westland Way, Woodstock *58*
Westmacott, Sir Richard 12
Wharf Farm, Eynsham *69*
Wharf Stream, Eynsham 70
White, Gilbert 24
Whitehill Wood 53

Wido de Oileio 40
William the Conqueror 40
Winchombe Abbey 29
Windrush, River 6, 29
Witney *64*
"Wold Without End" 8
Woodstock *58*, *64*
Wootton 56, *58*
Wychwood Forest
     7, 8, 41, 44, 48, *57*, *61*
Wytham Wood *69*

Y

Yantell, or Yantle, River 25
"Year with the Birds, A" *25*

The quiet evening kept her tryst:
Beneath an open sky we rode,
And passed into a wandering mist
Along the perfect Evenlode.

The tender Evenlode that makes
Her meadows hush to hear the sound
Of waters mingling in the brakes,
And binds my heart to English ground.

Hilaire Belloc